This coloring book belongs to:

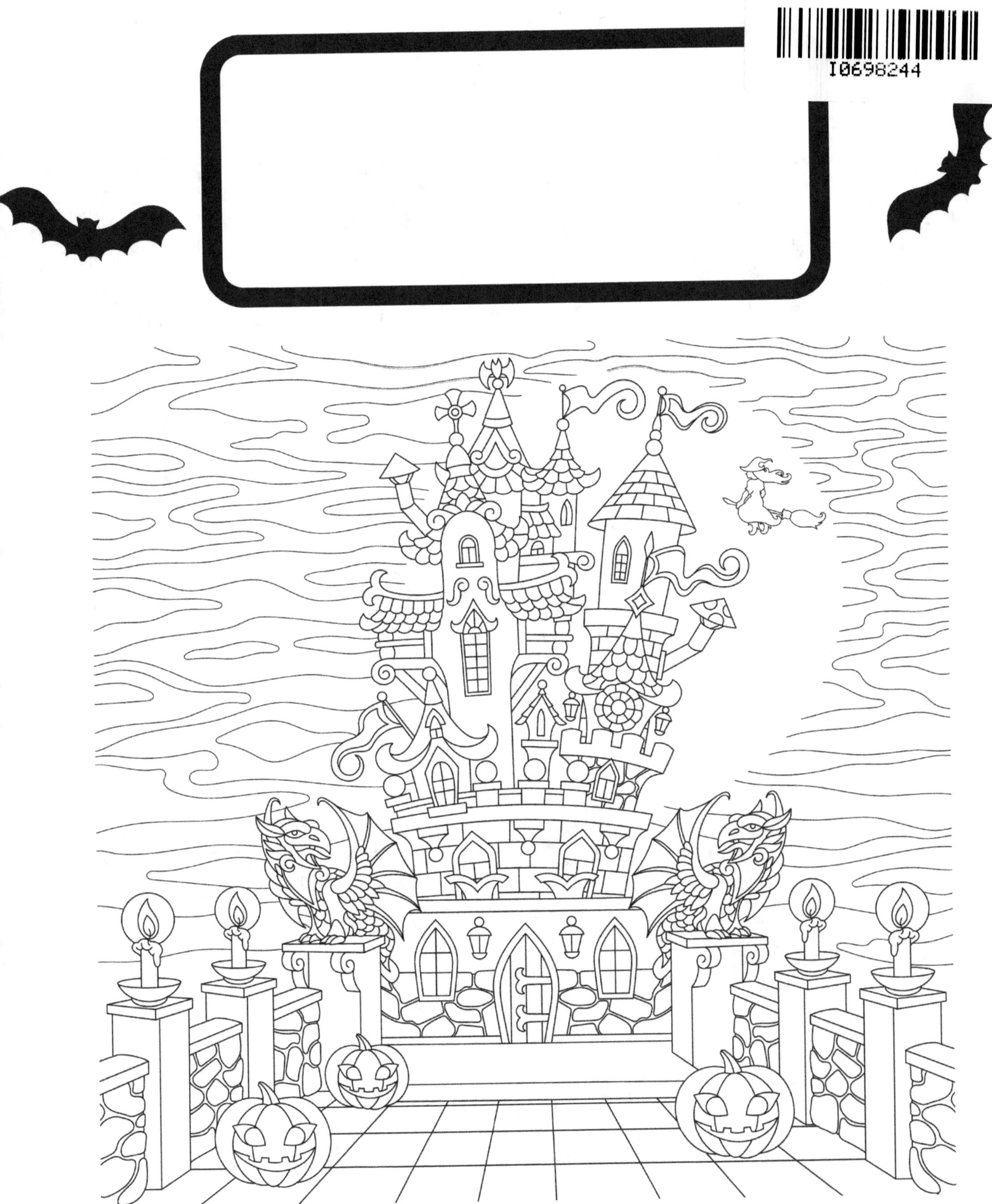

Color test

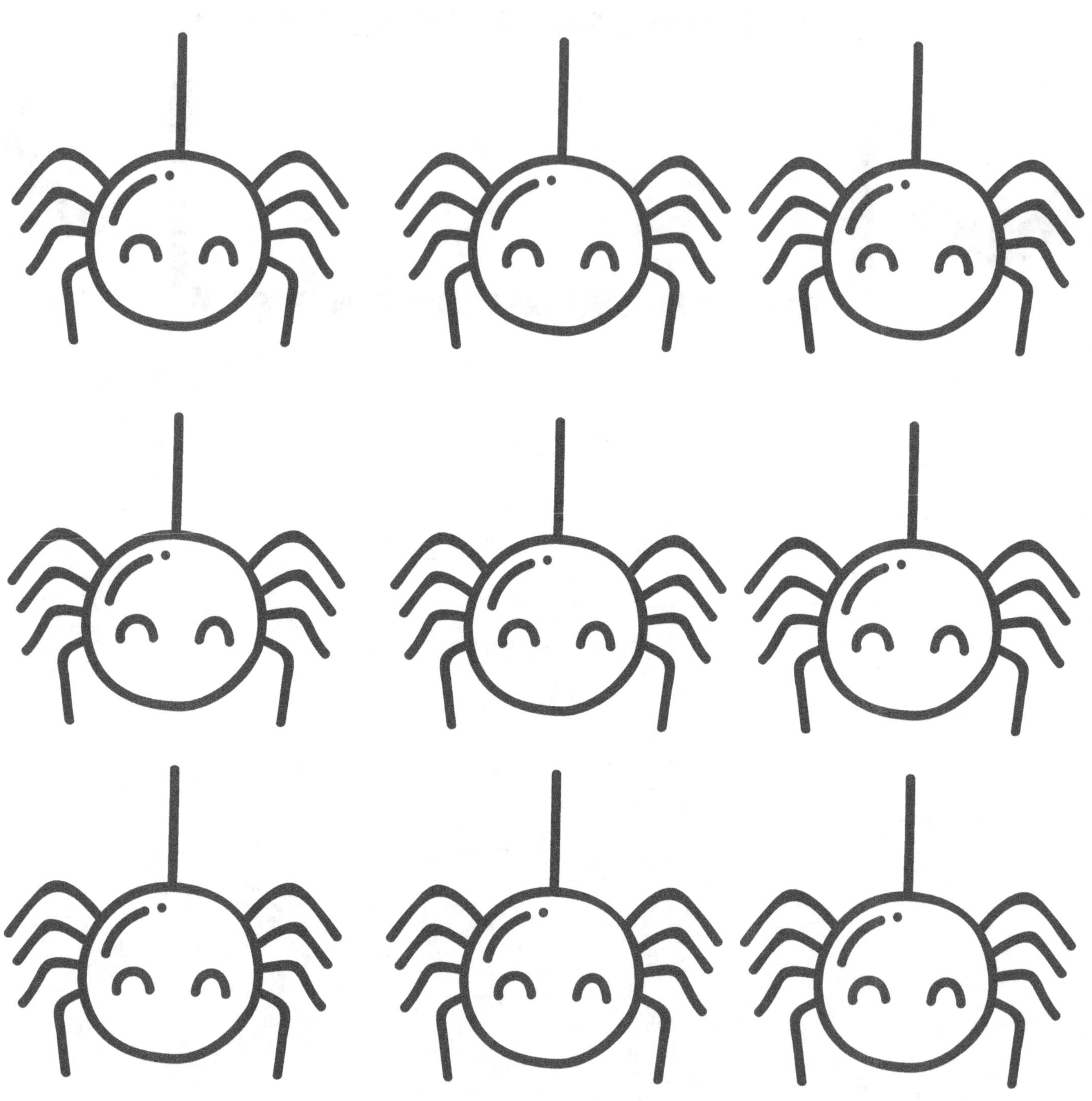

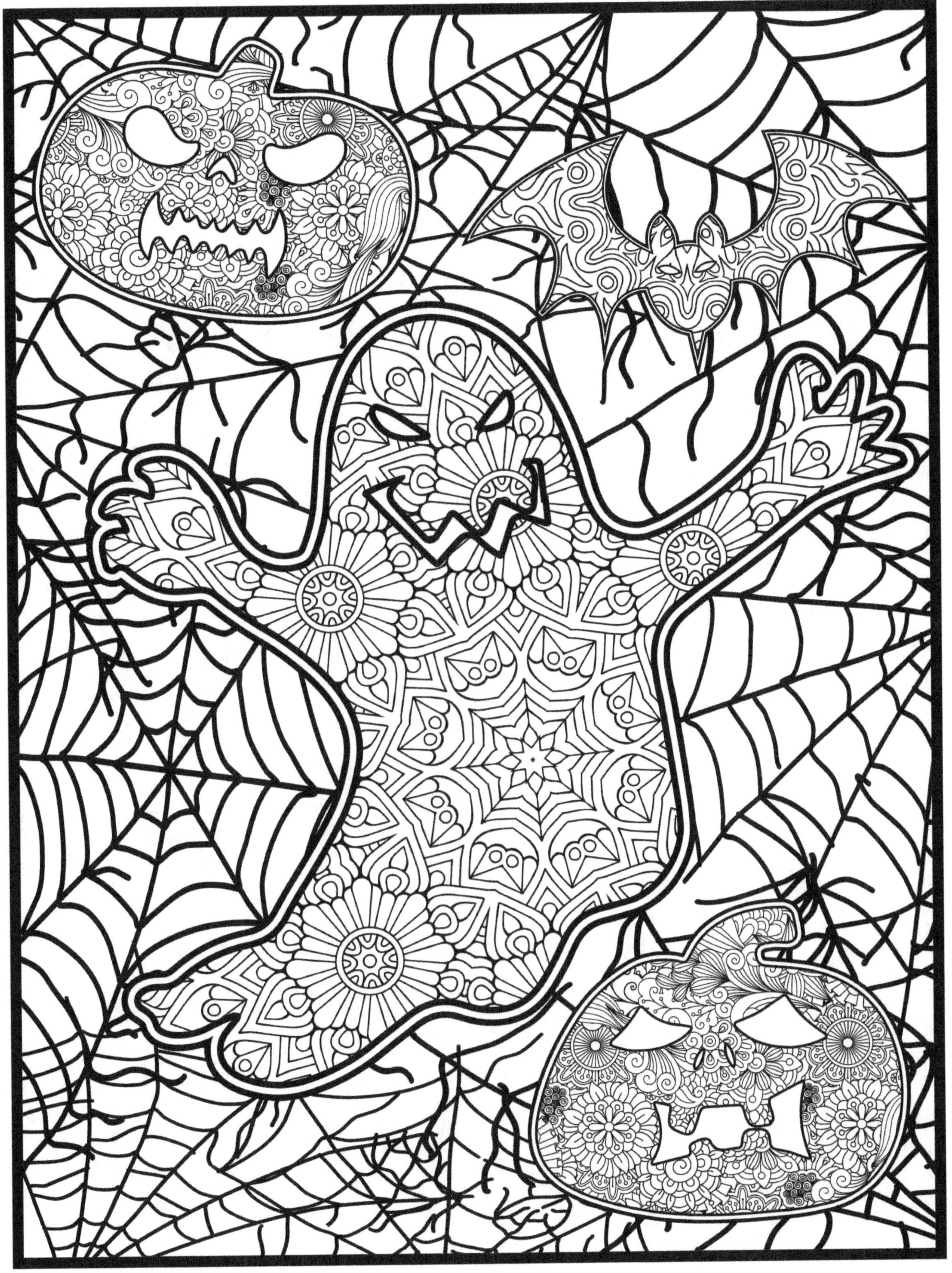

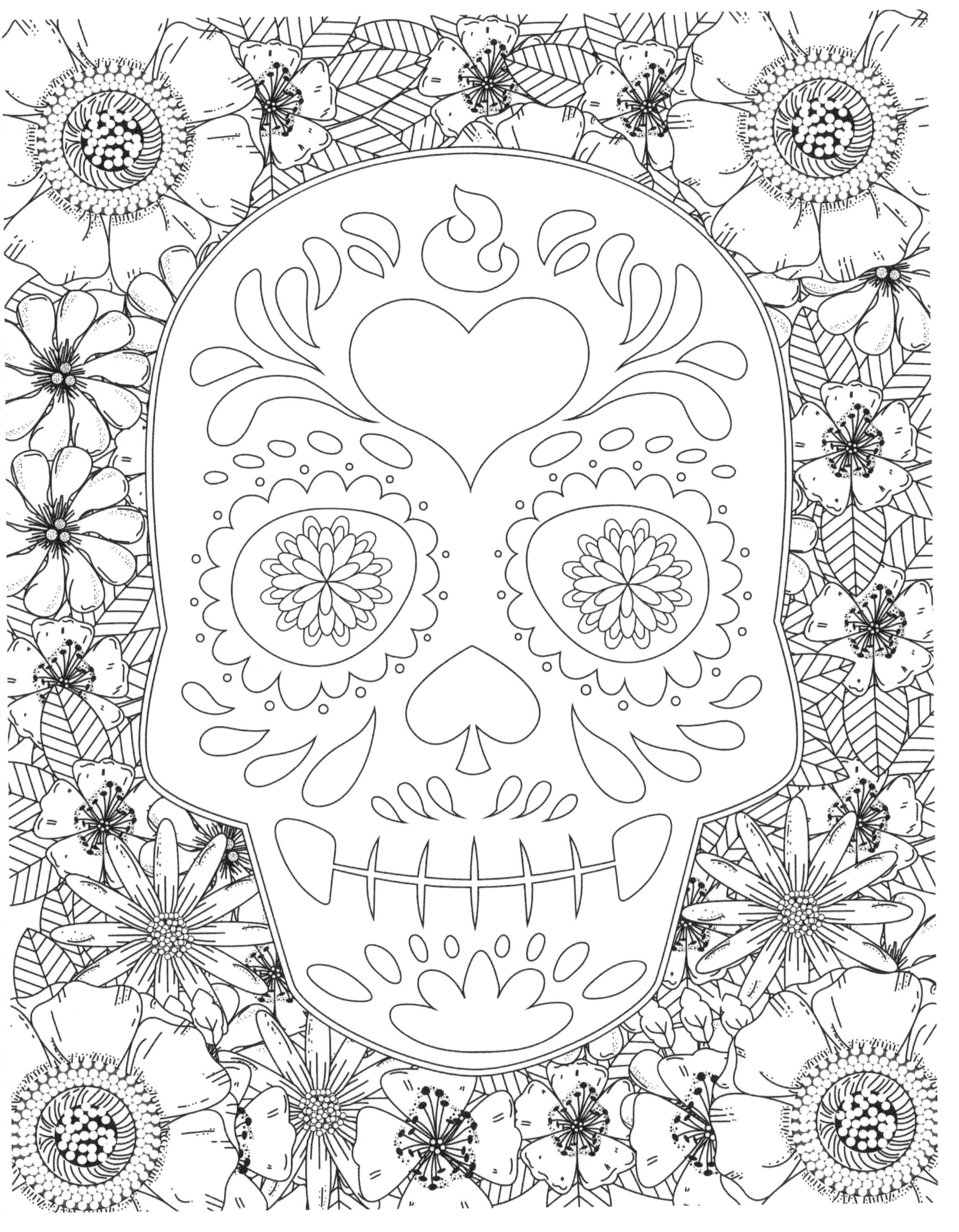

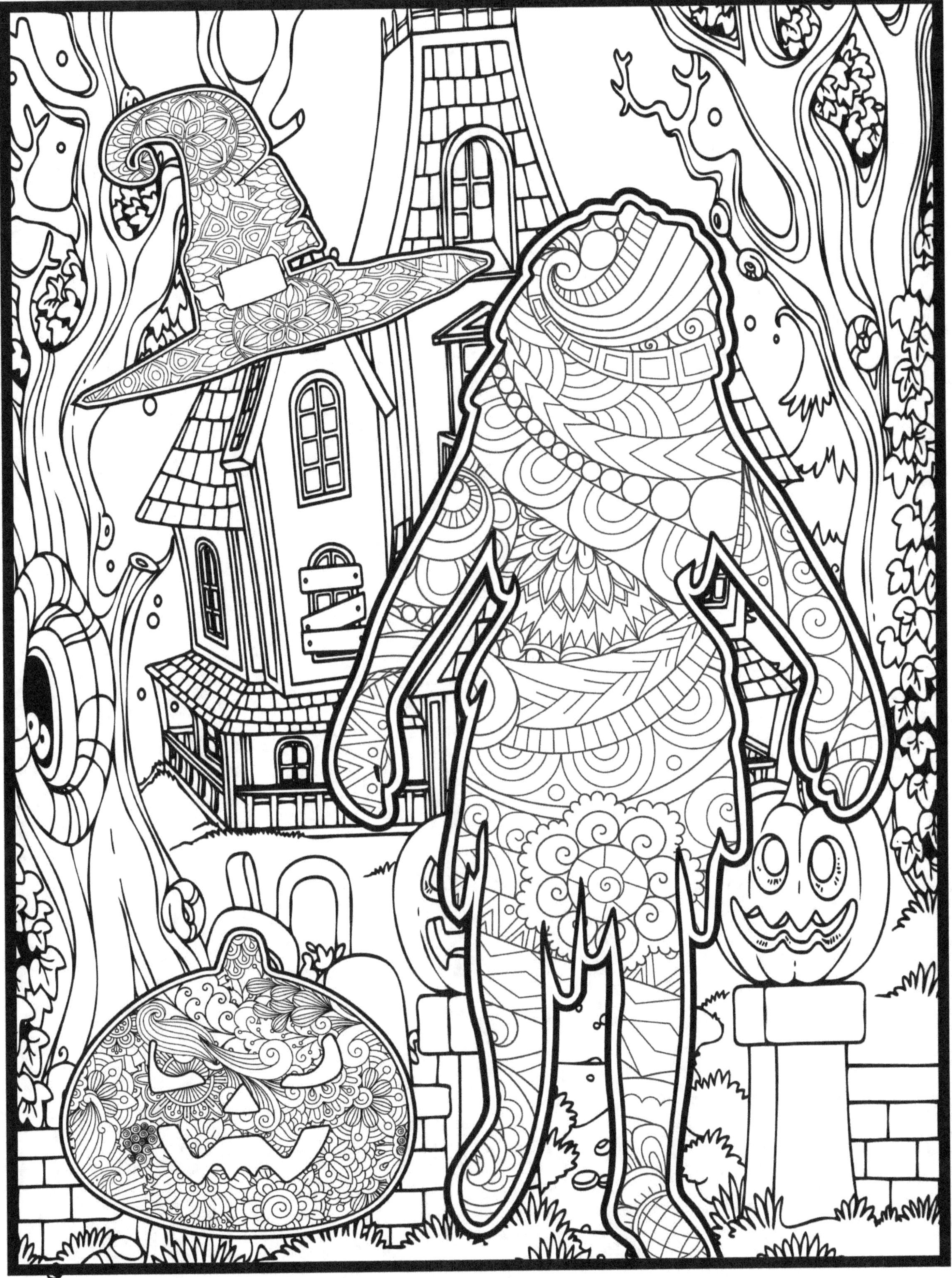

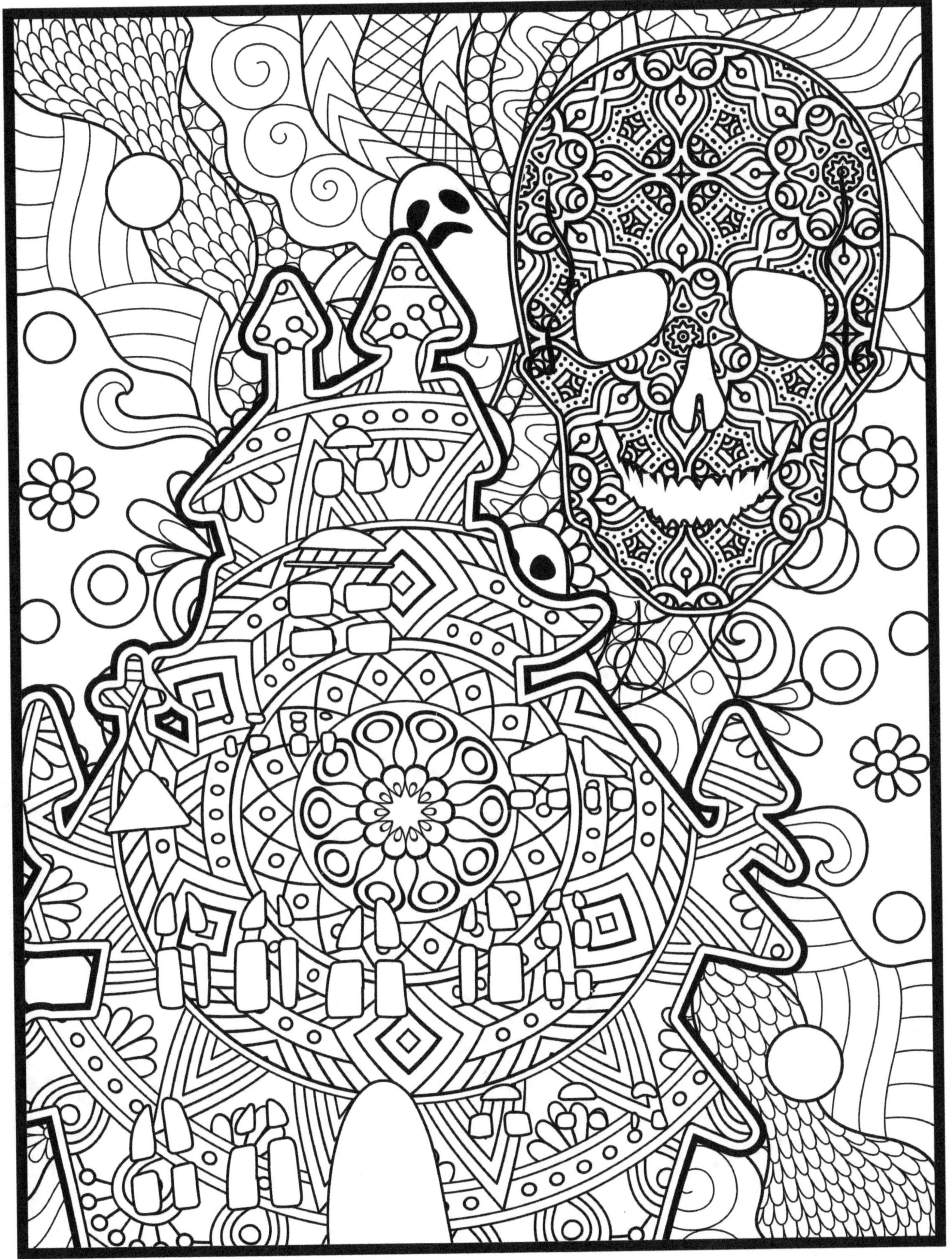

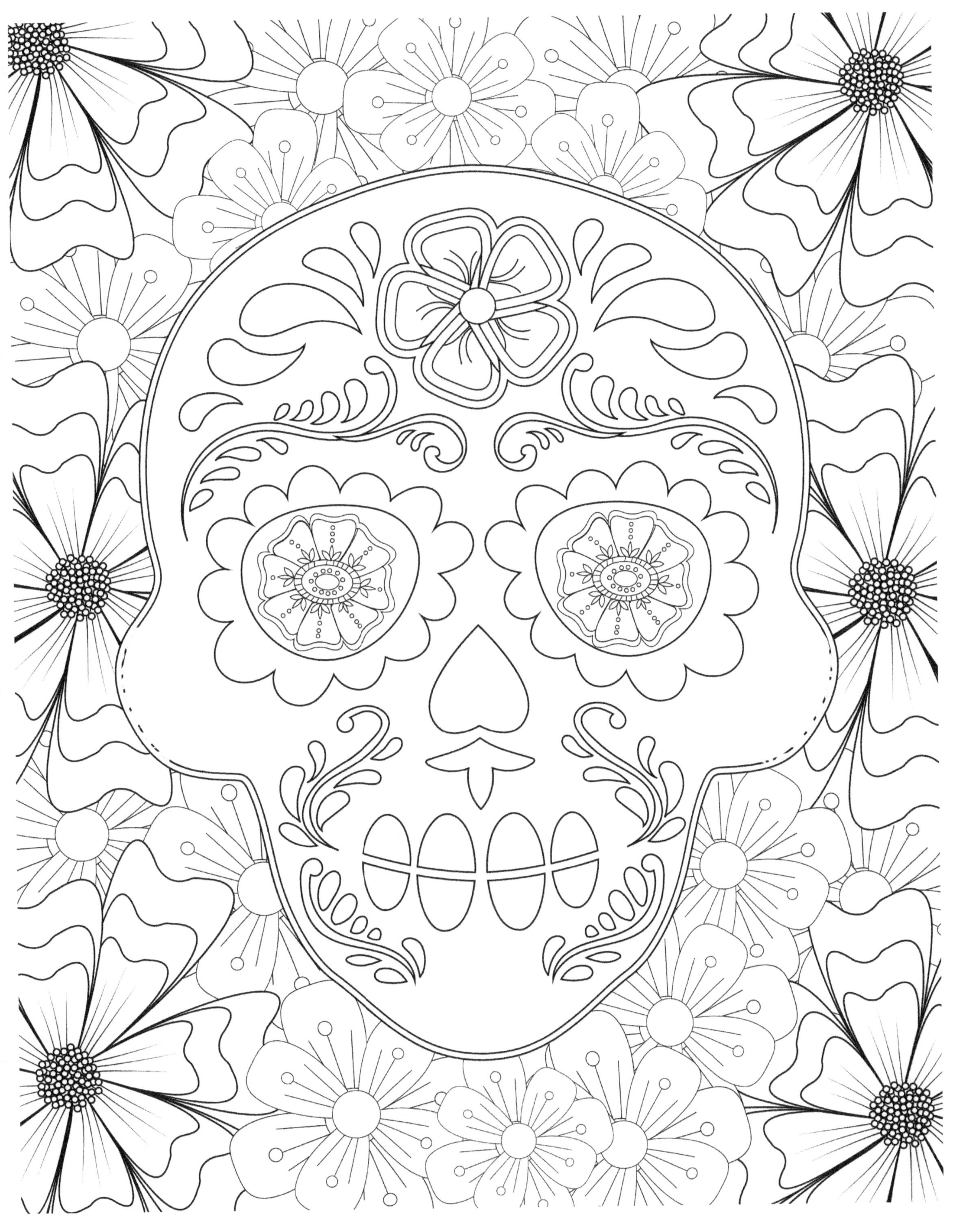

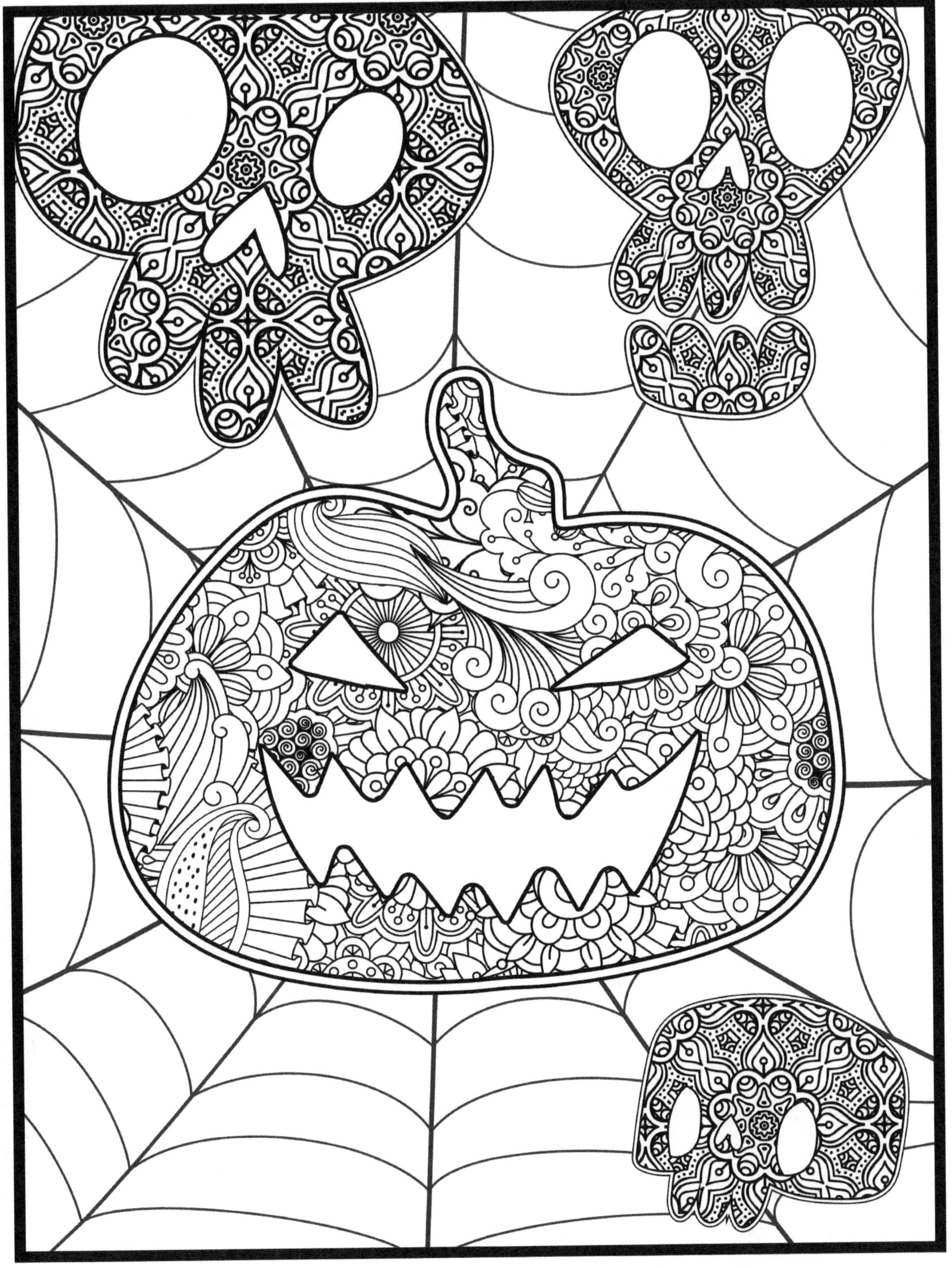

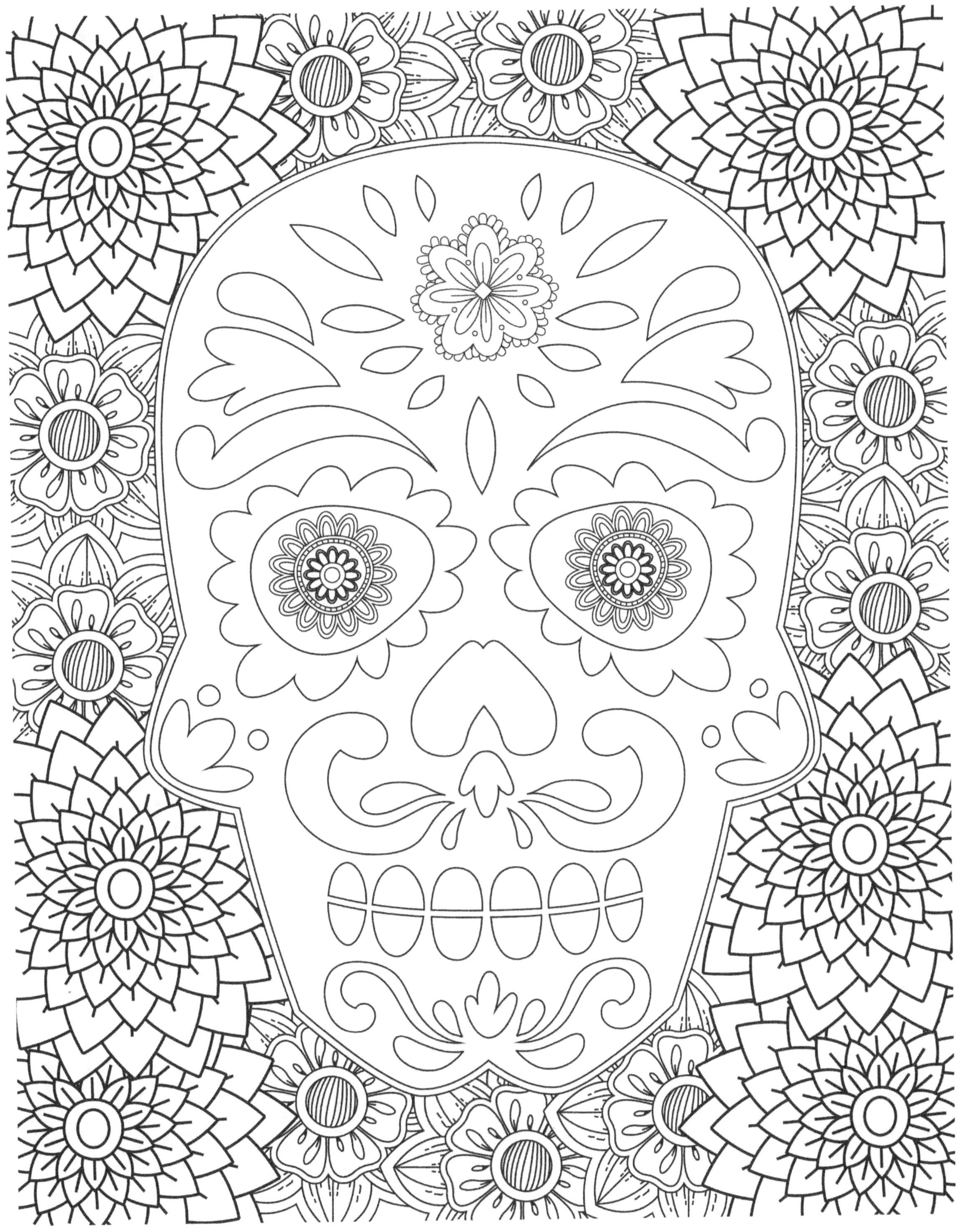

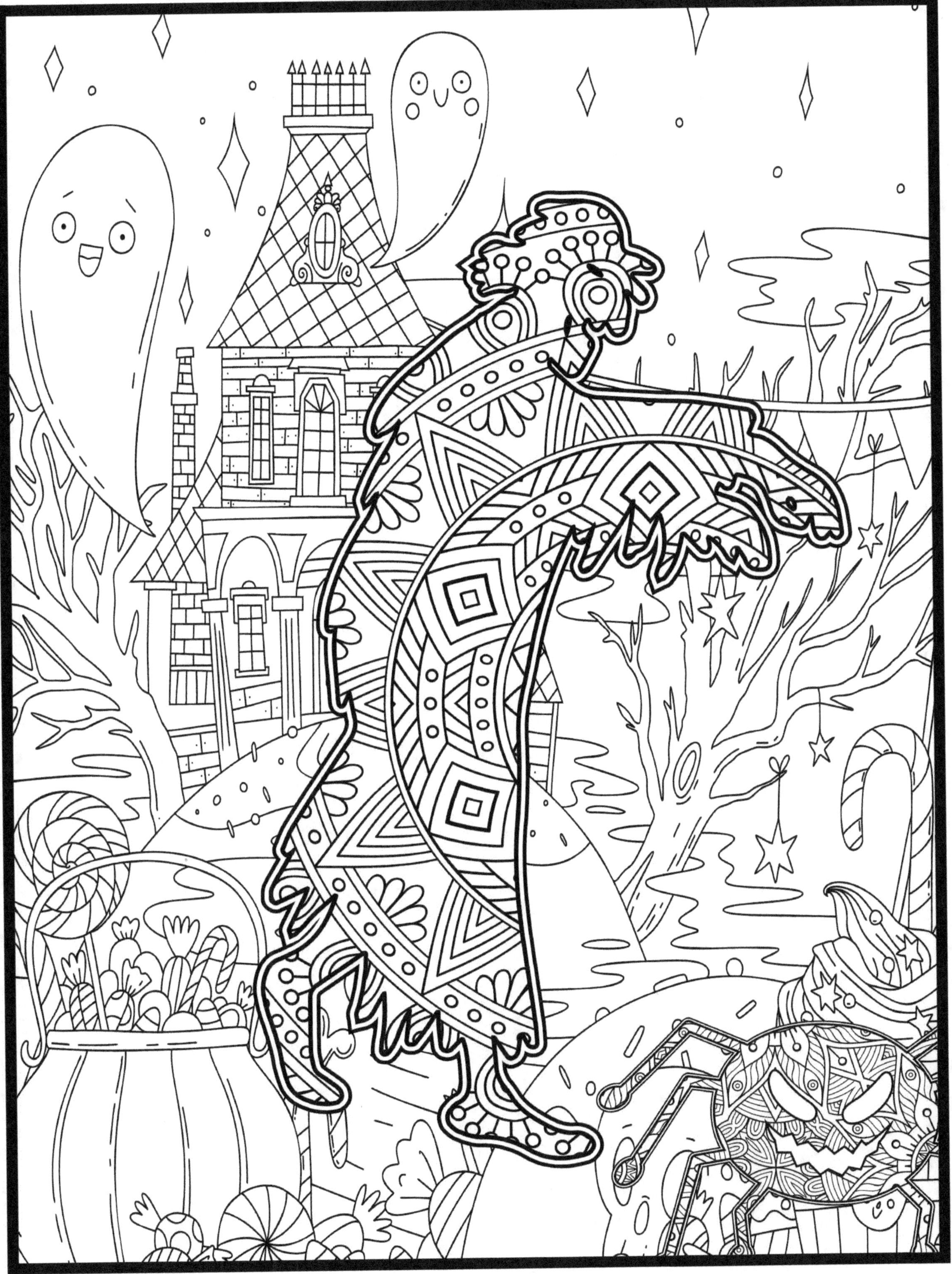

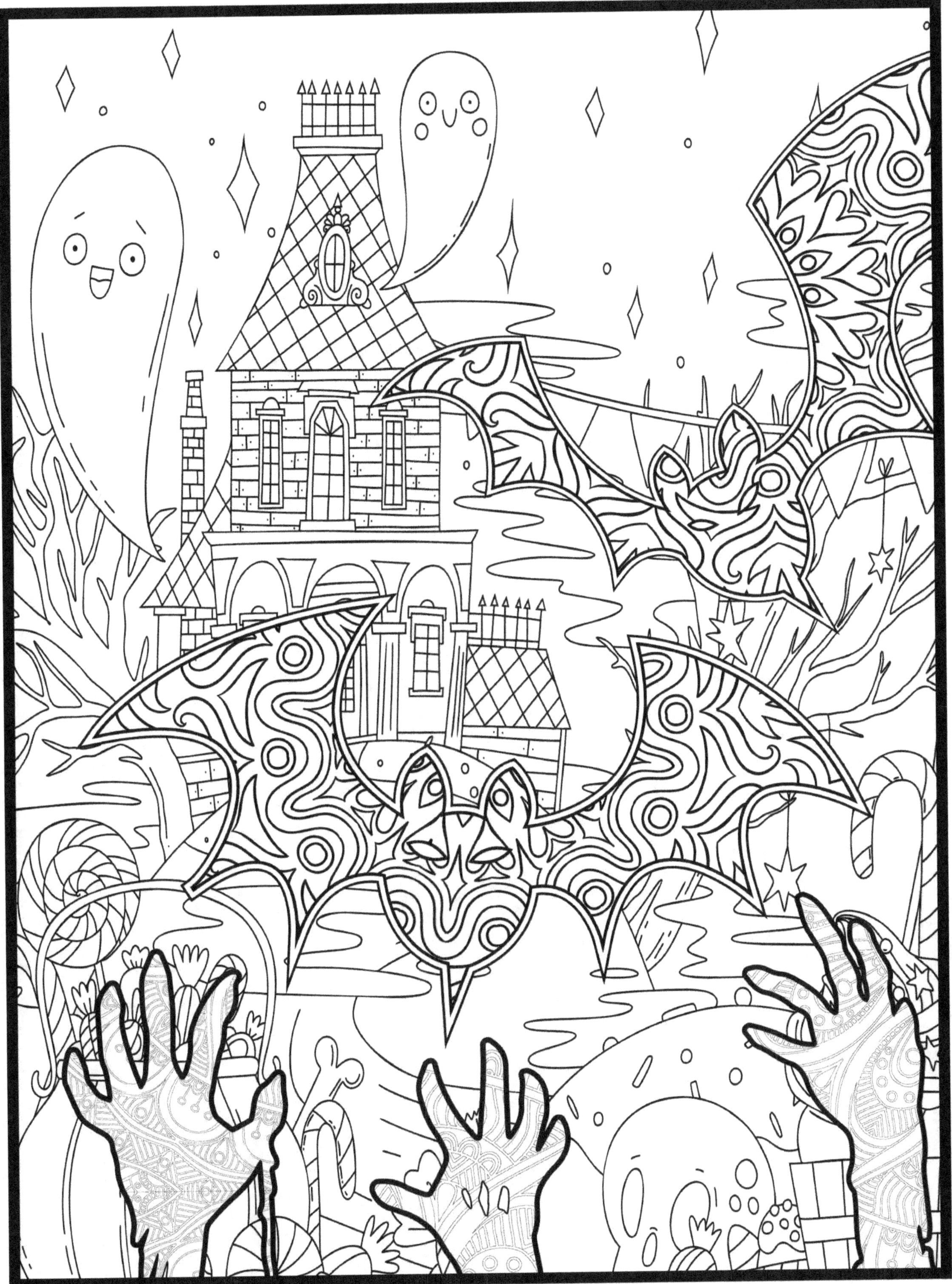

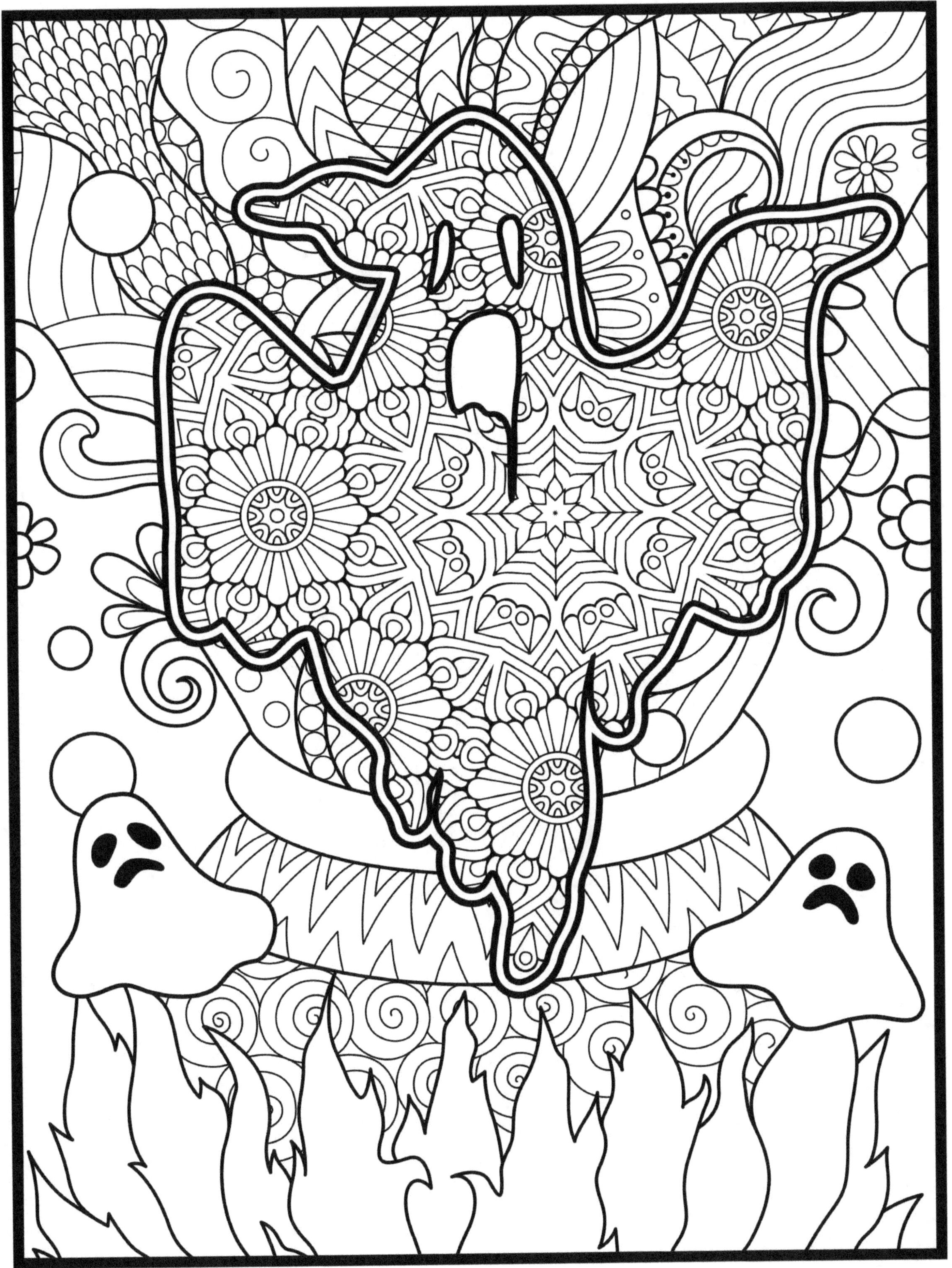

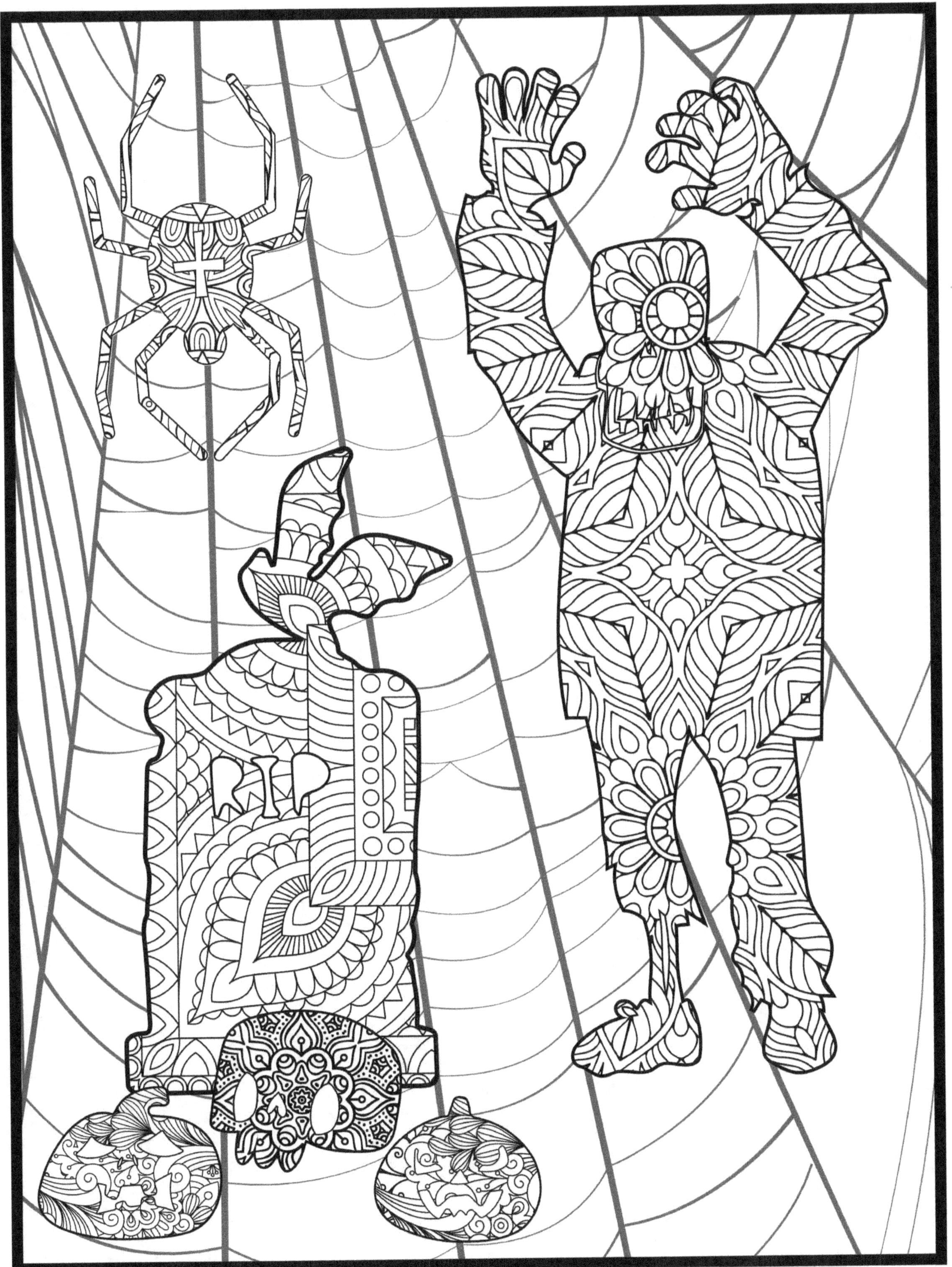

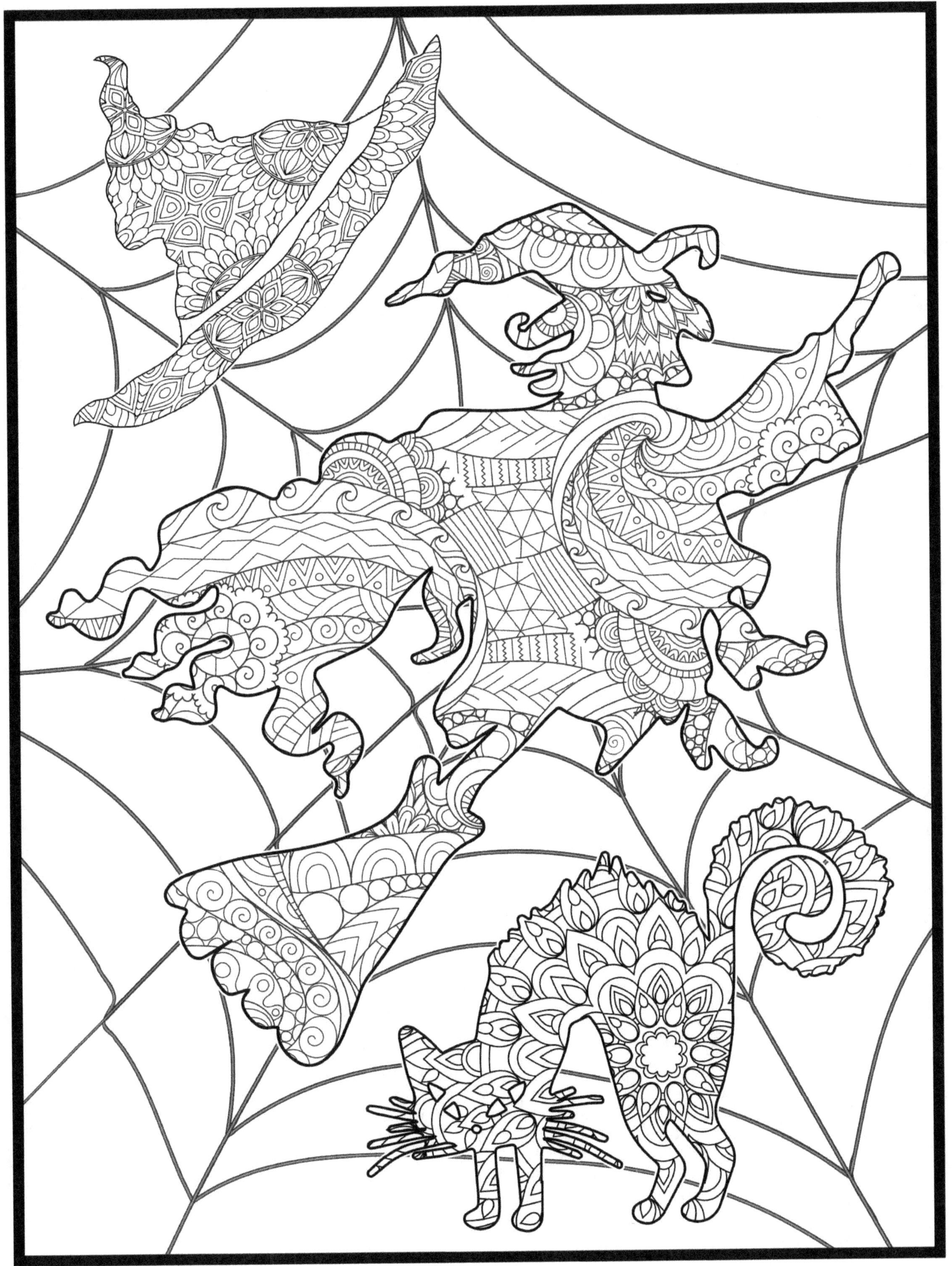

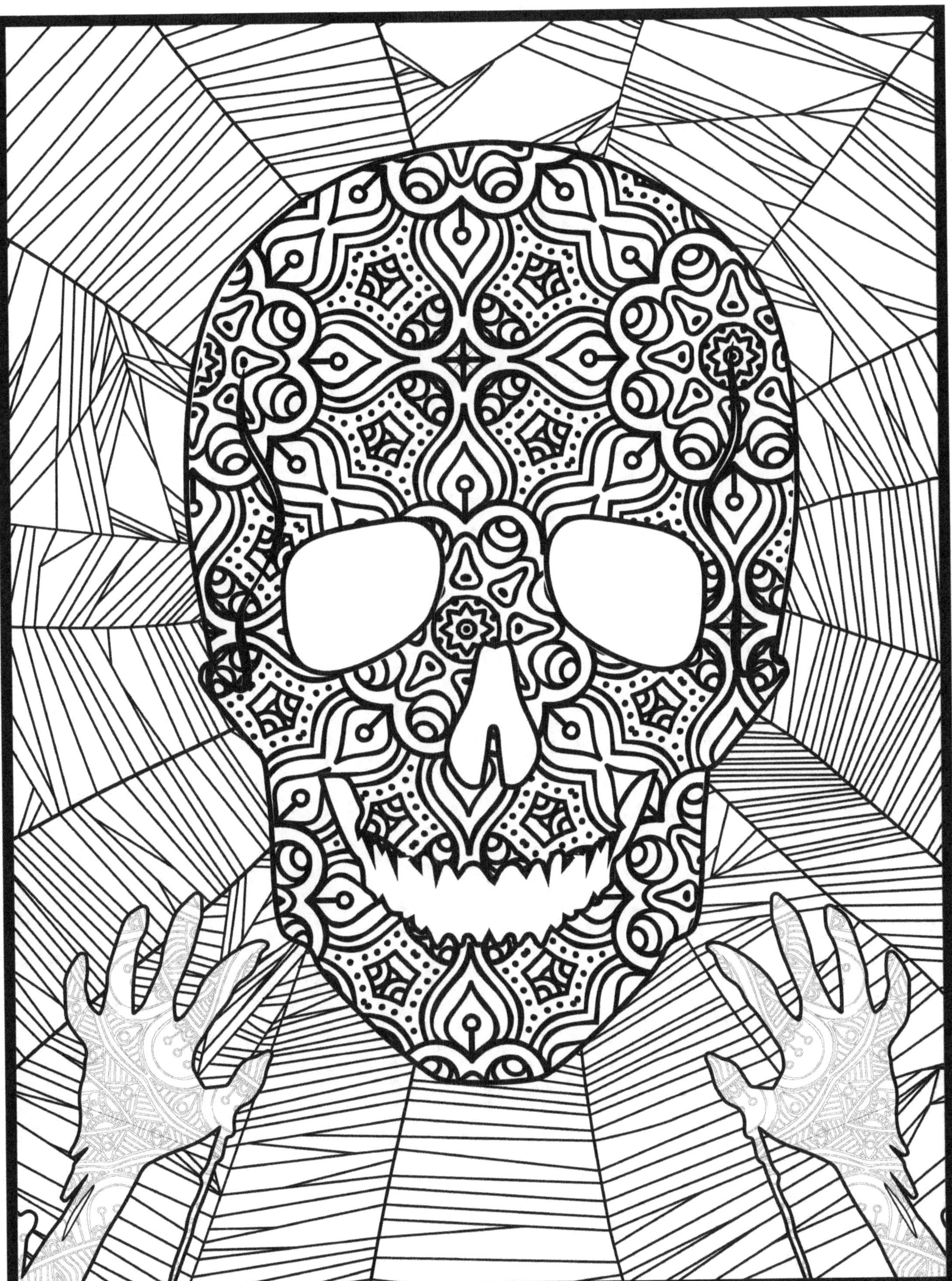

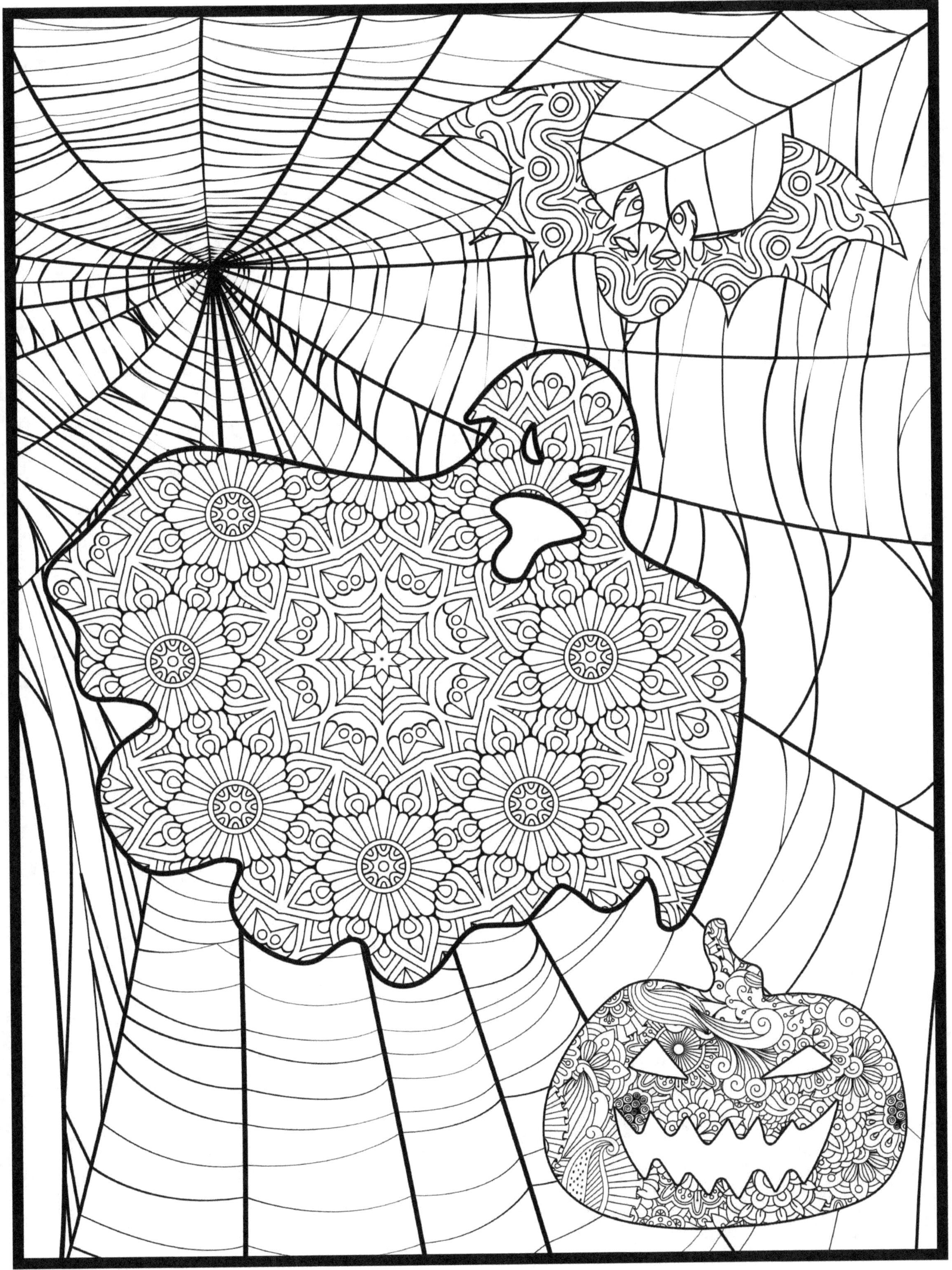

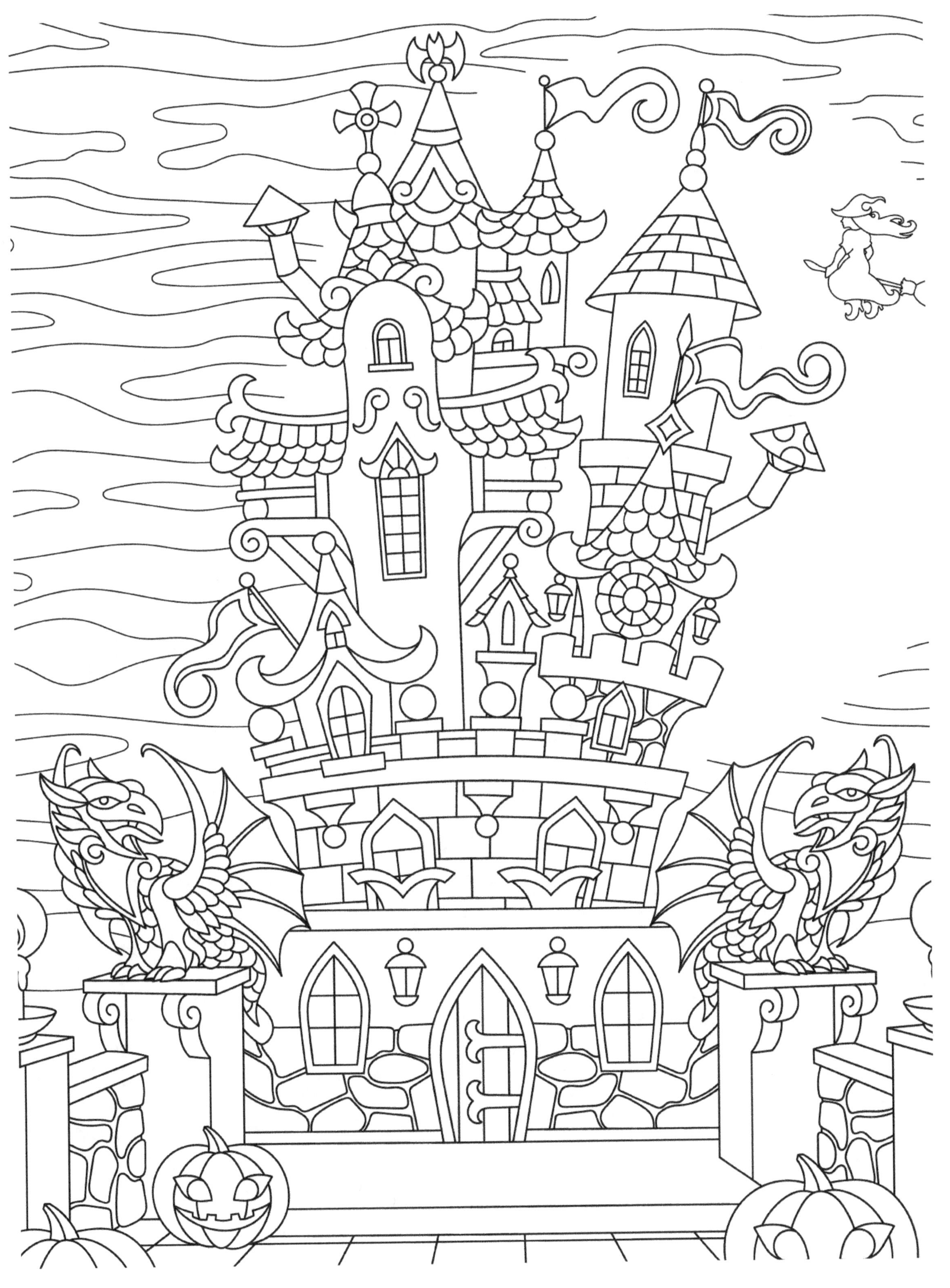

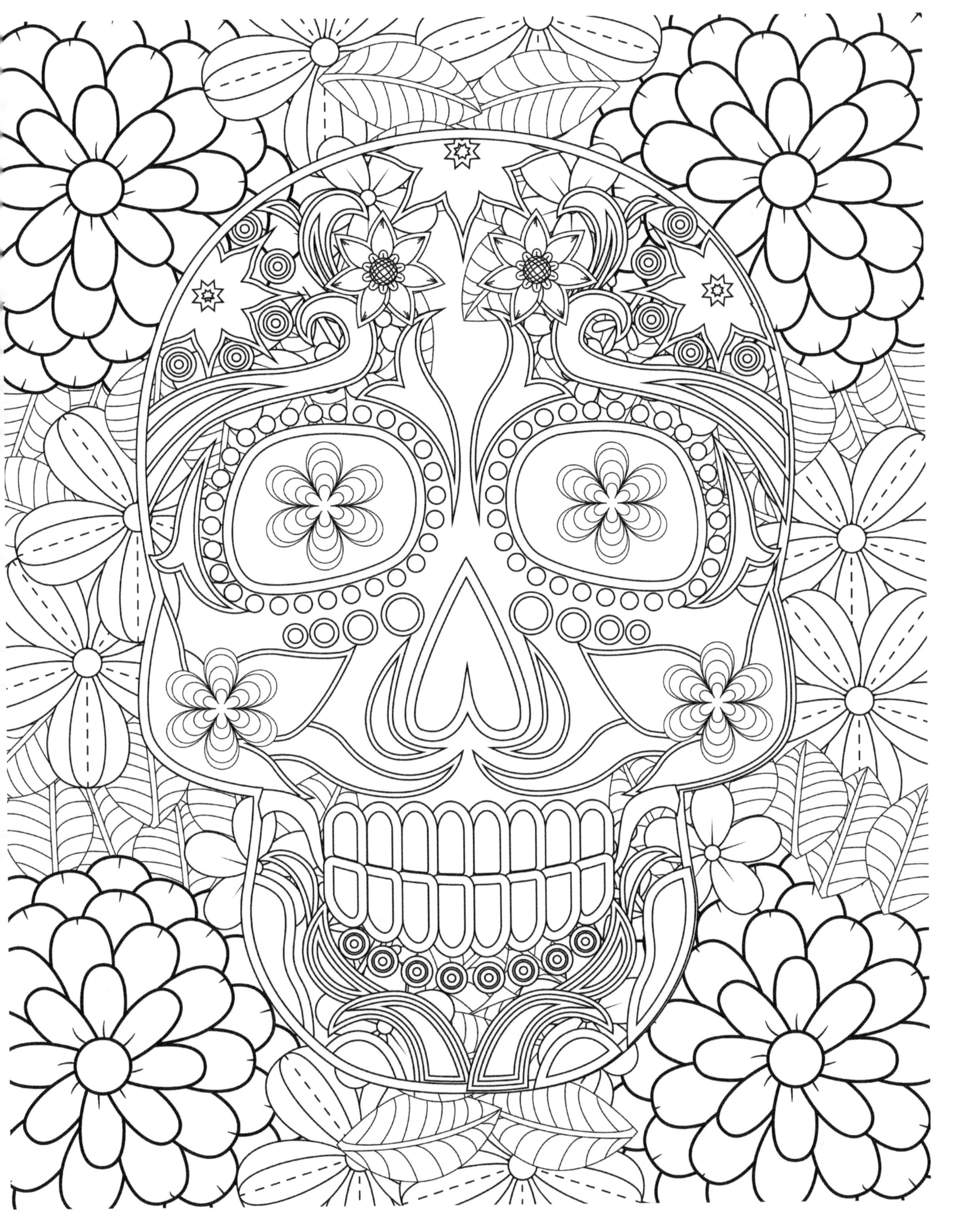

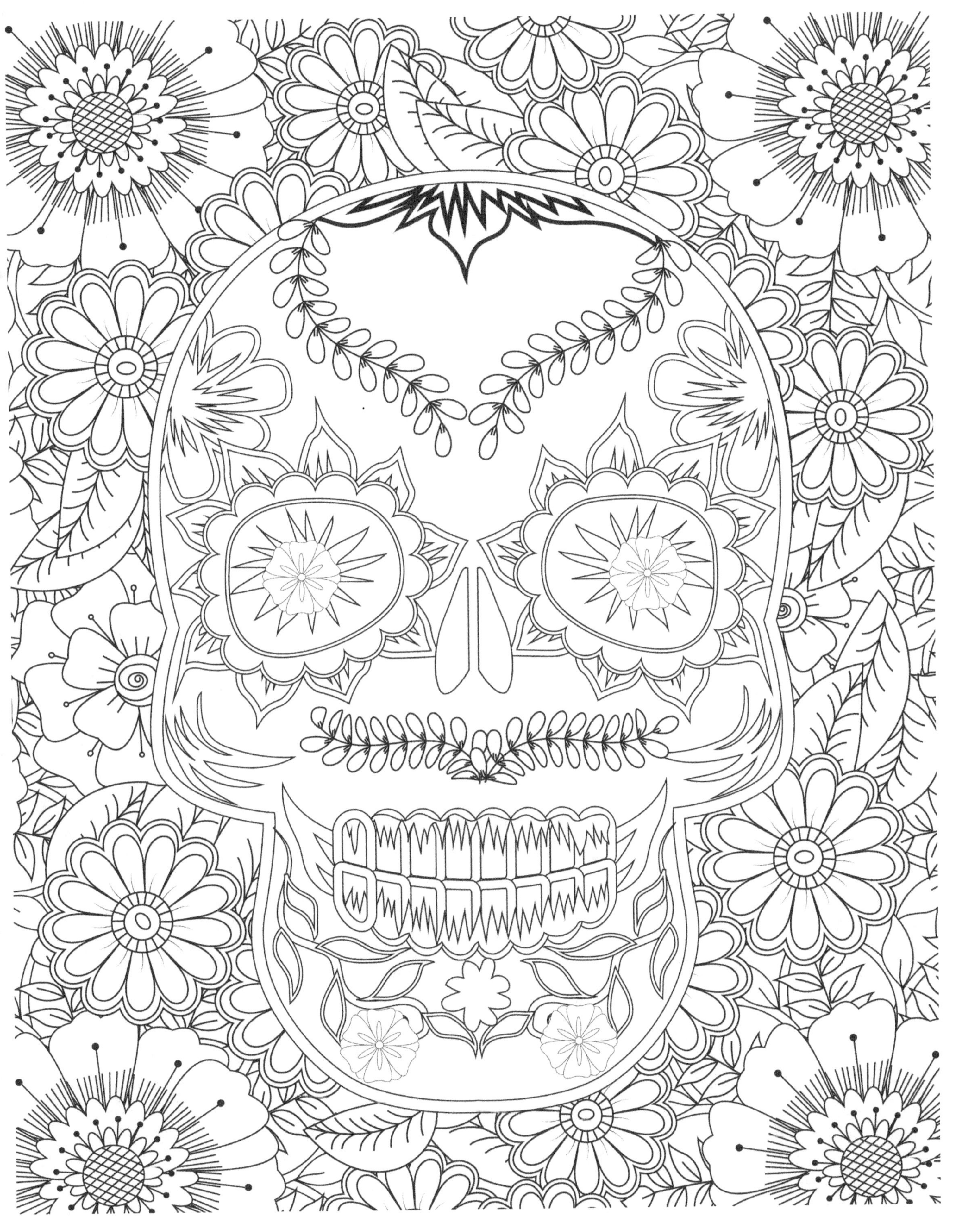

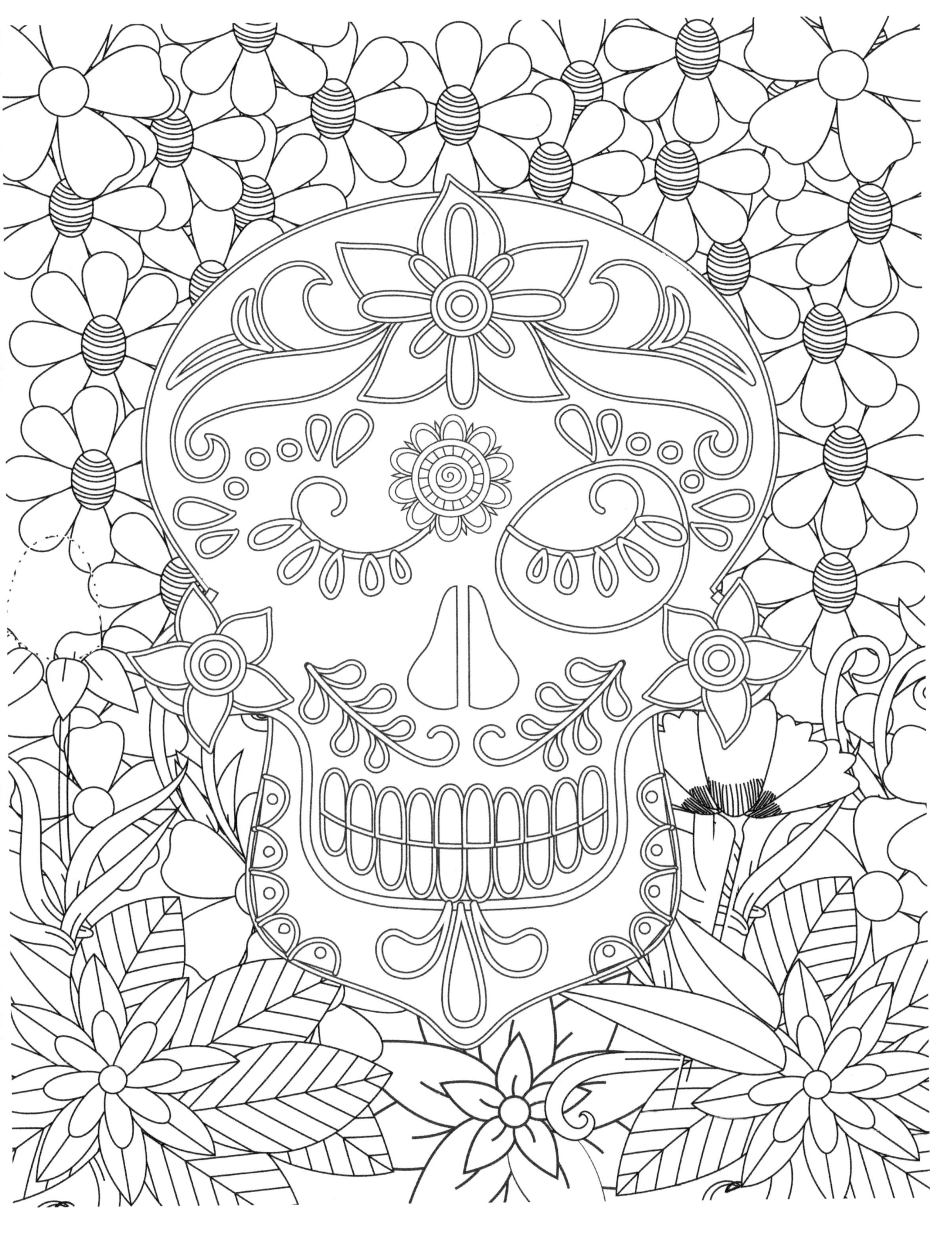

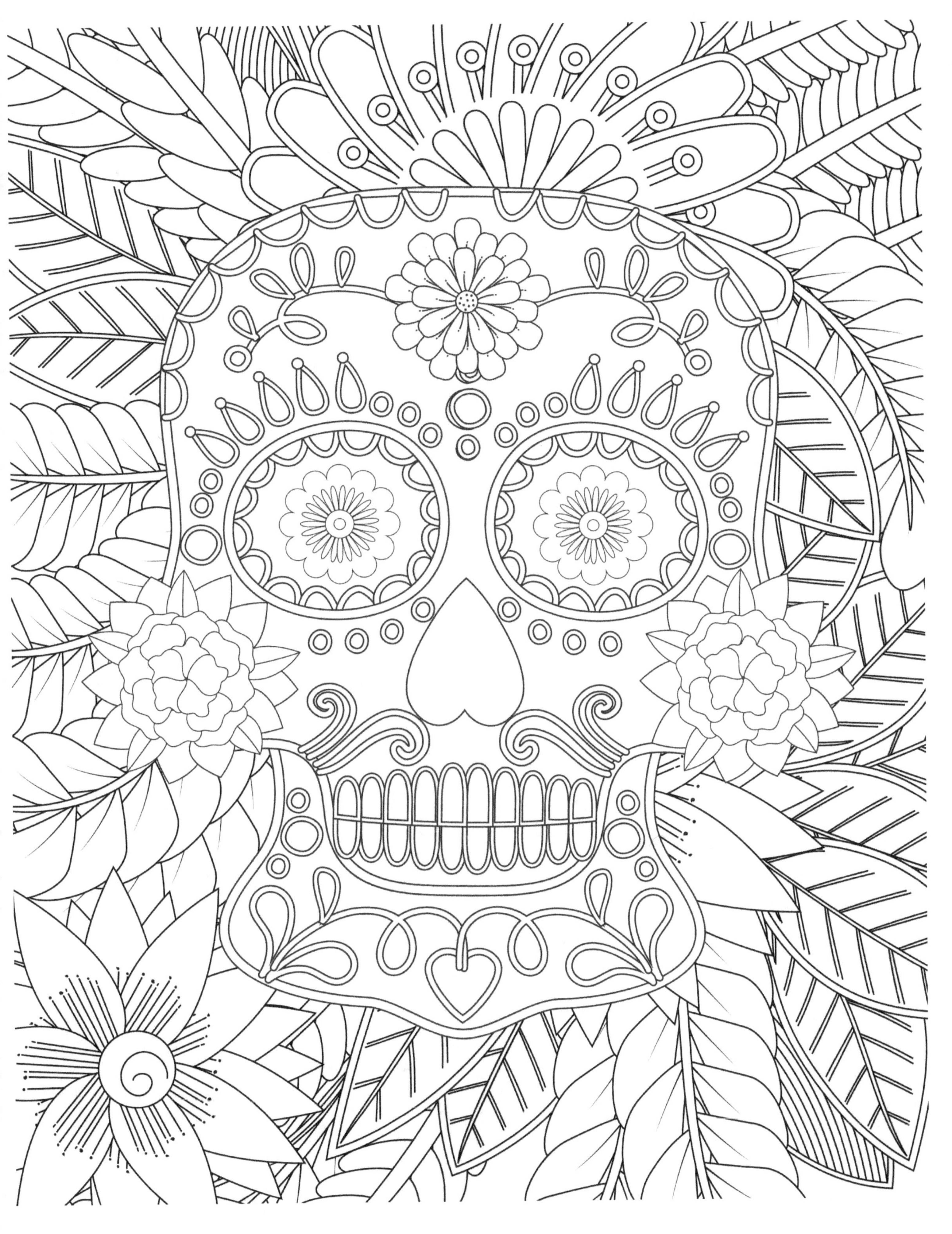

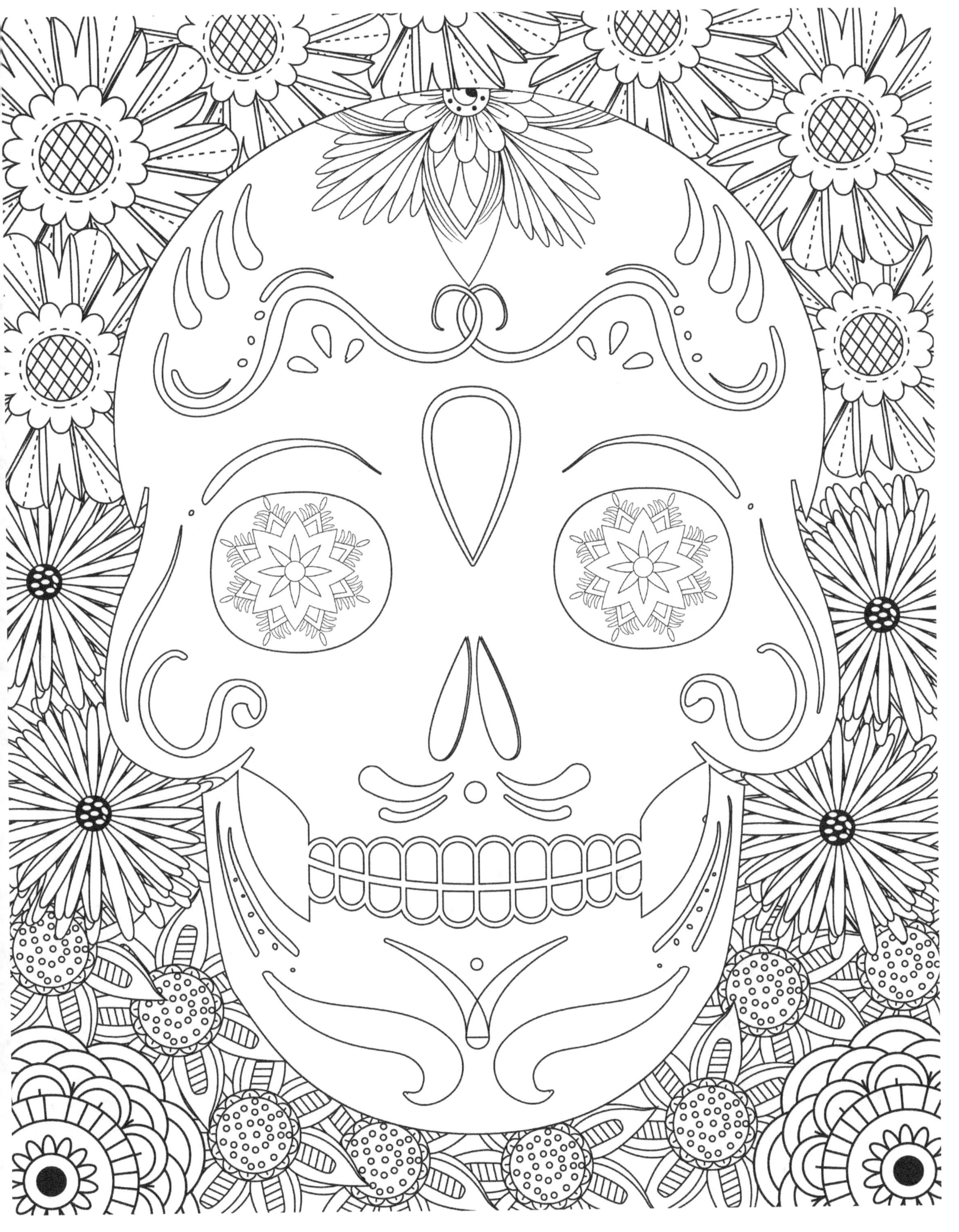

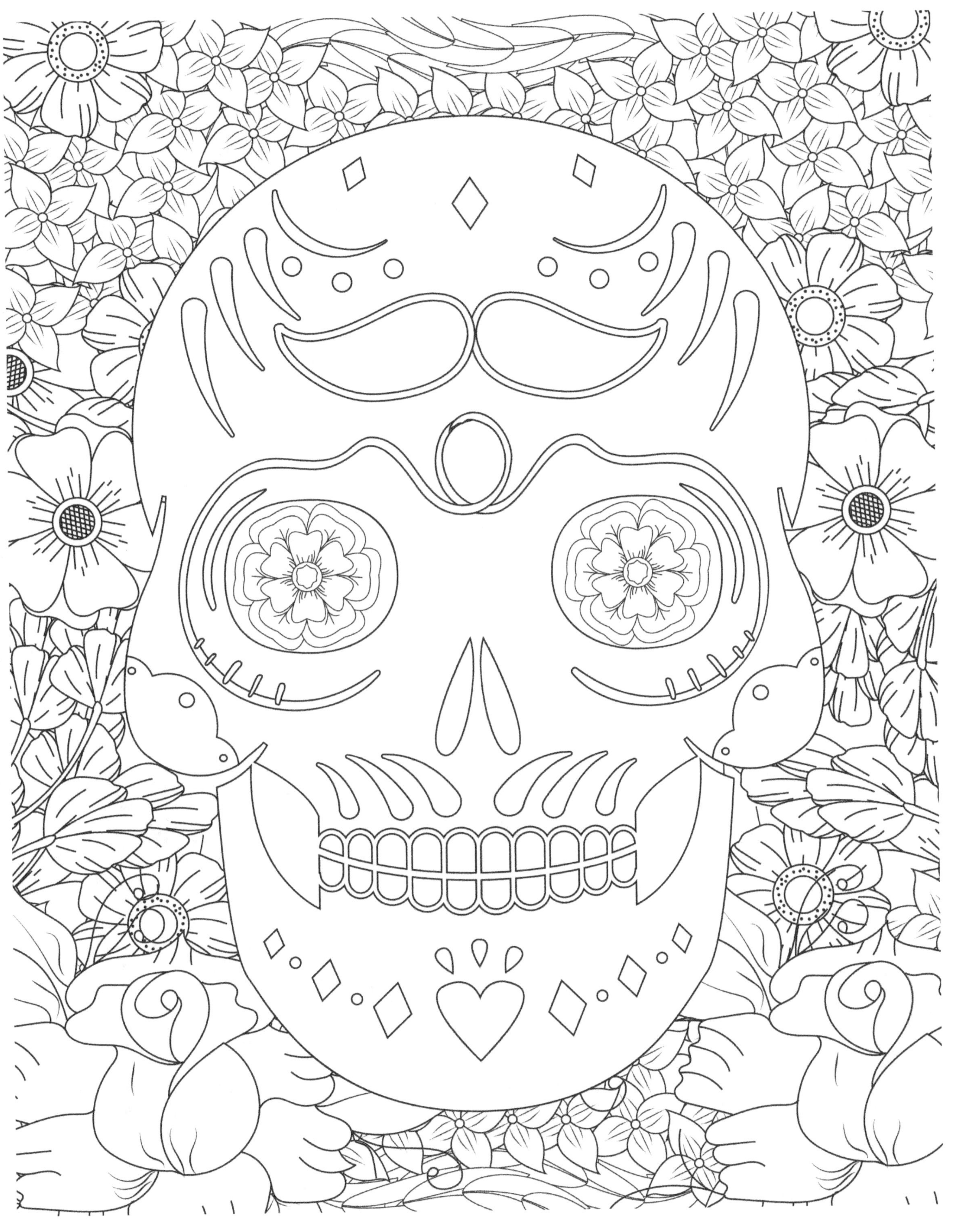

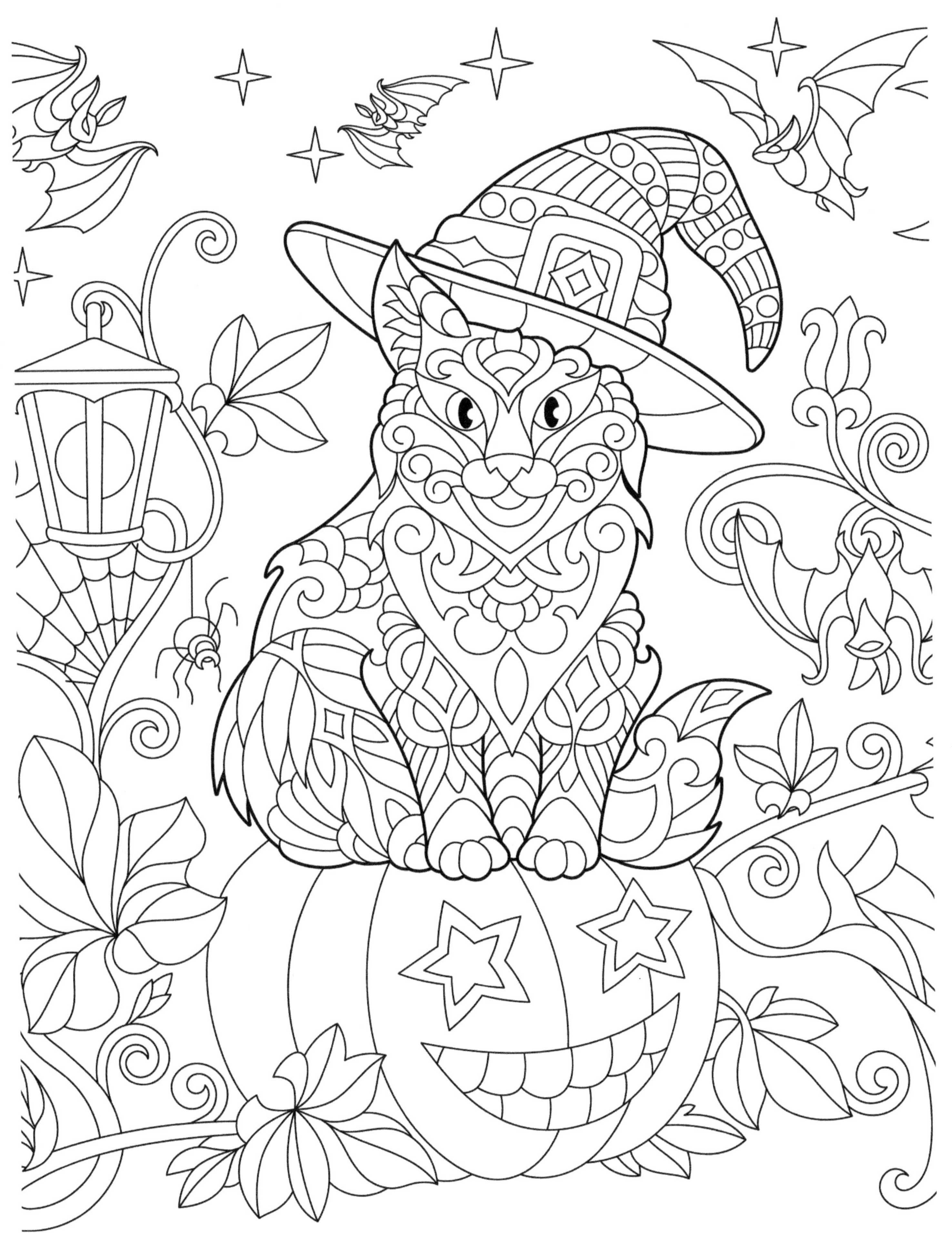

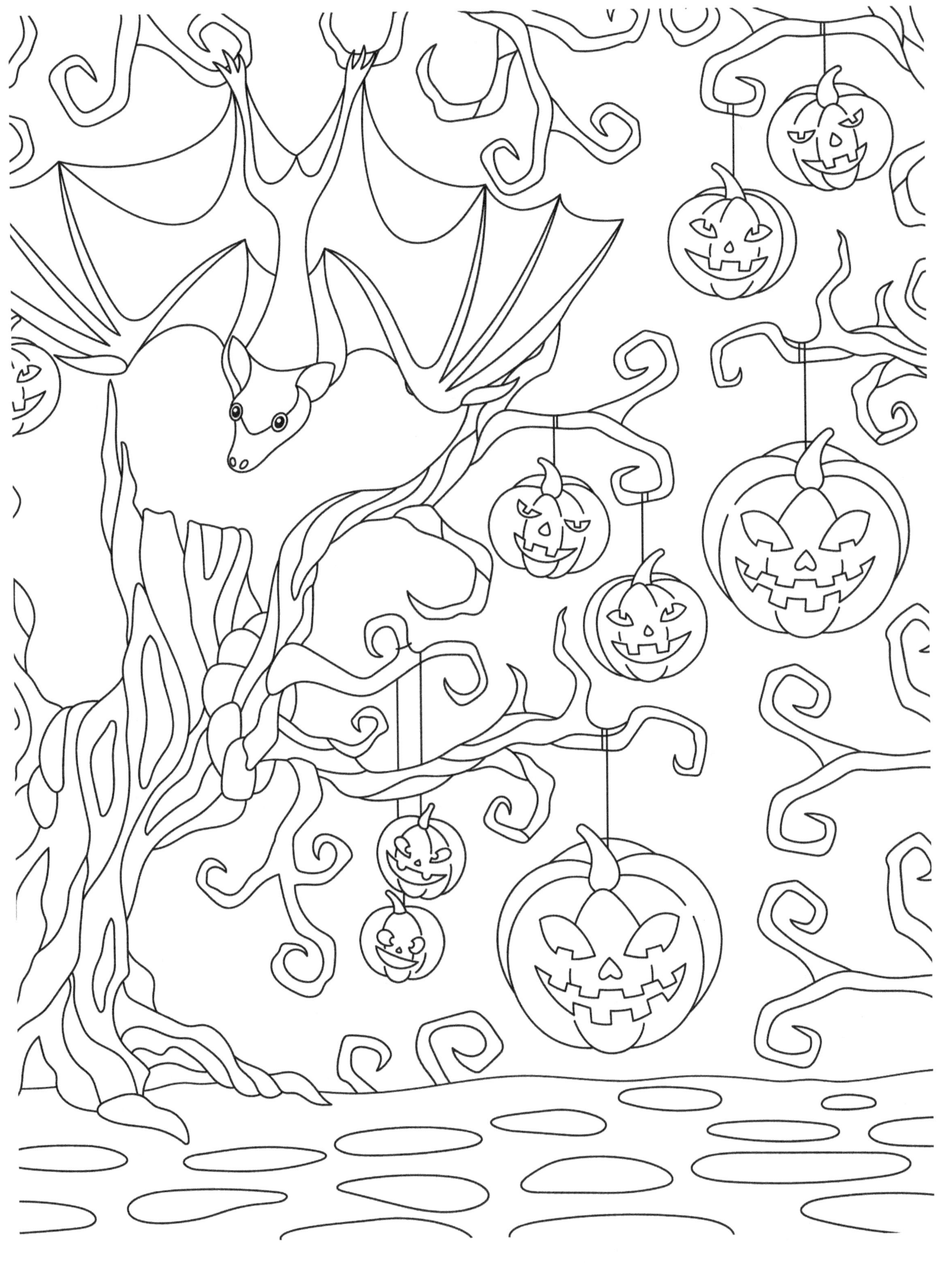

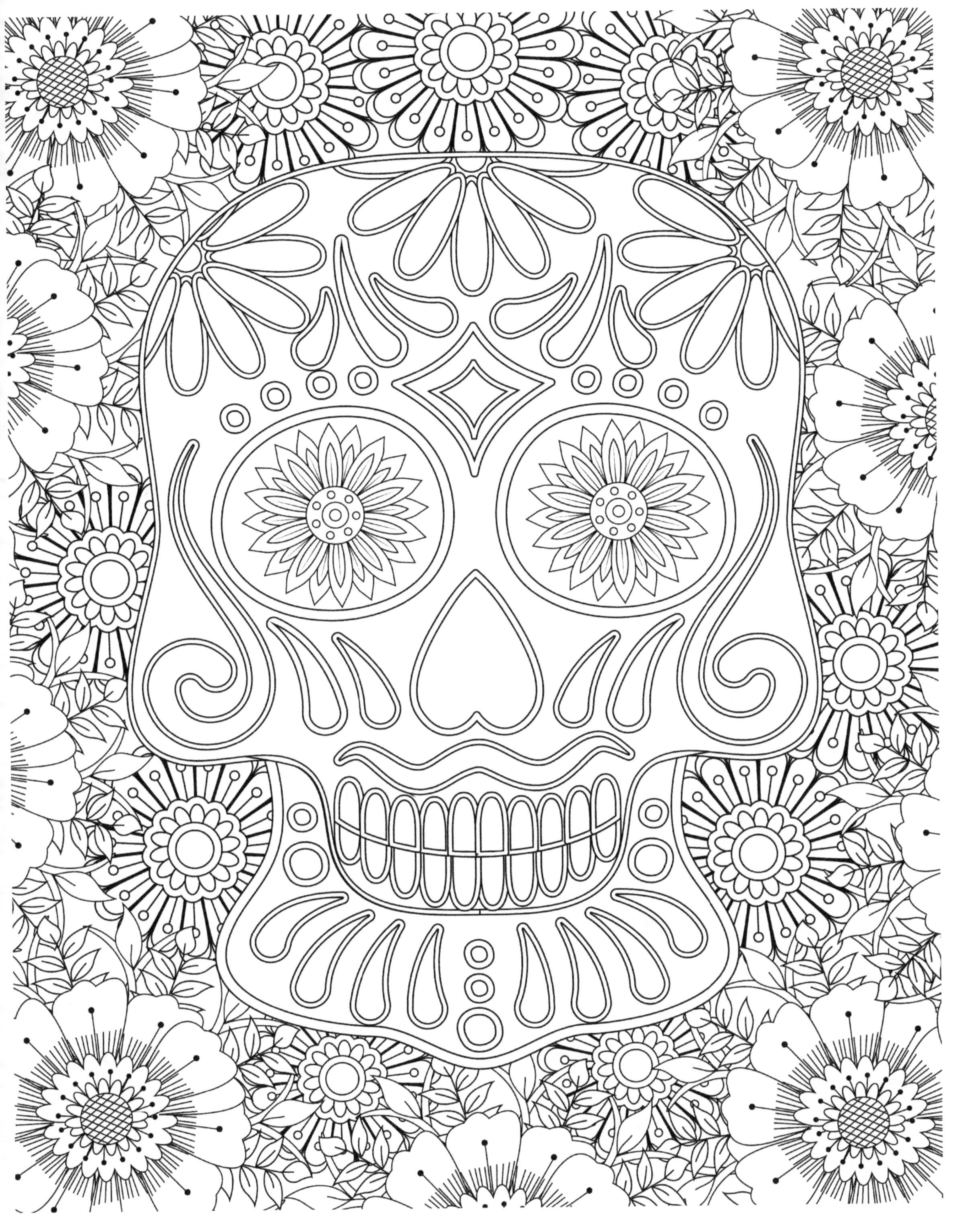

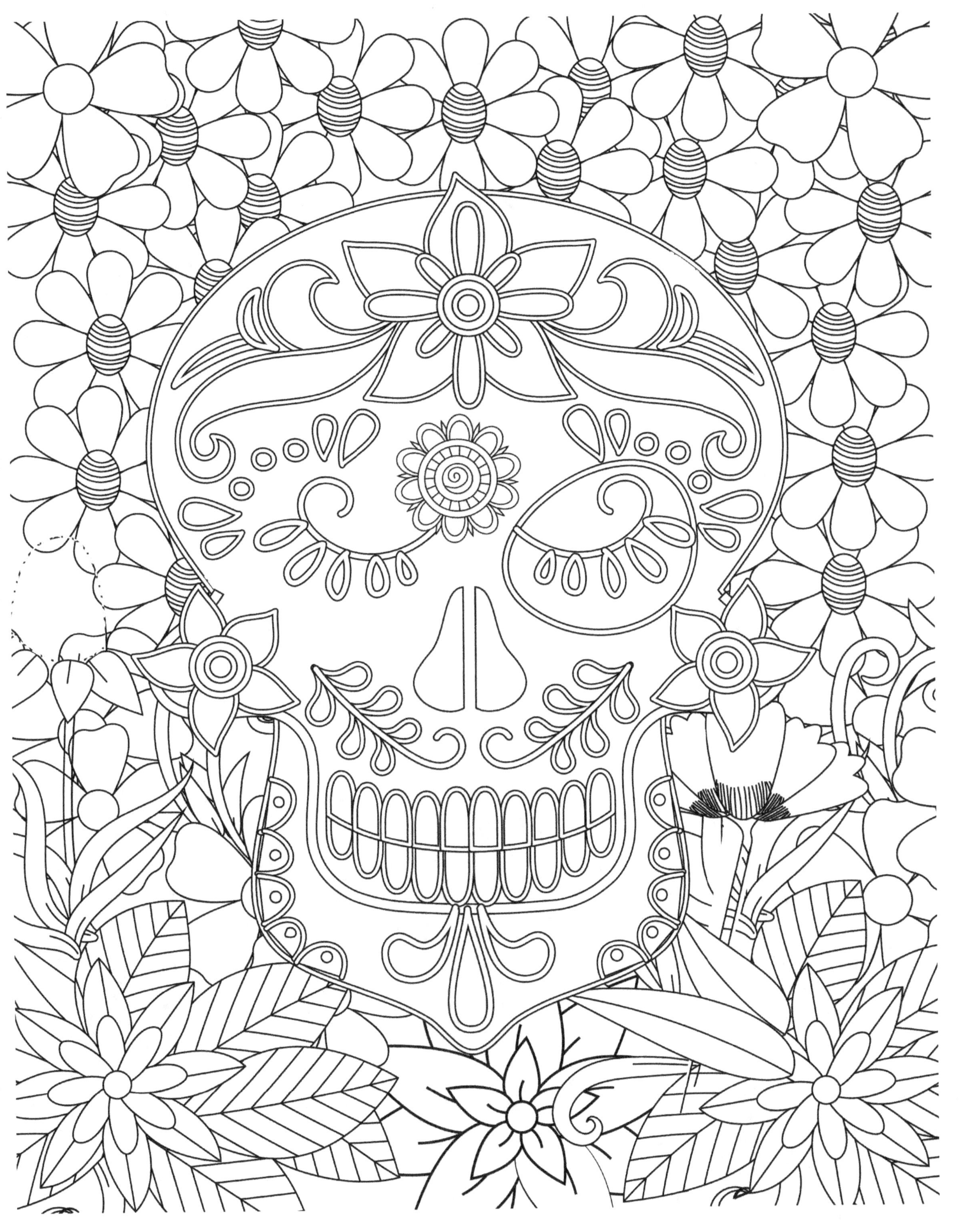

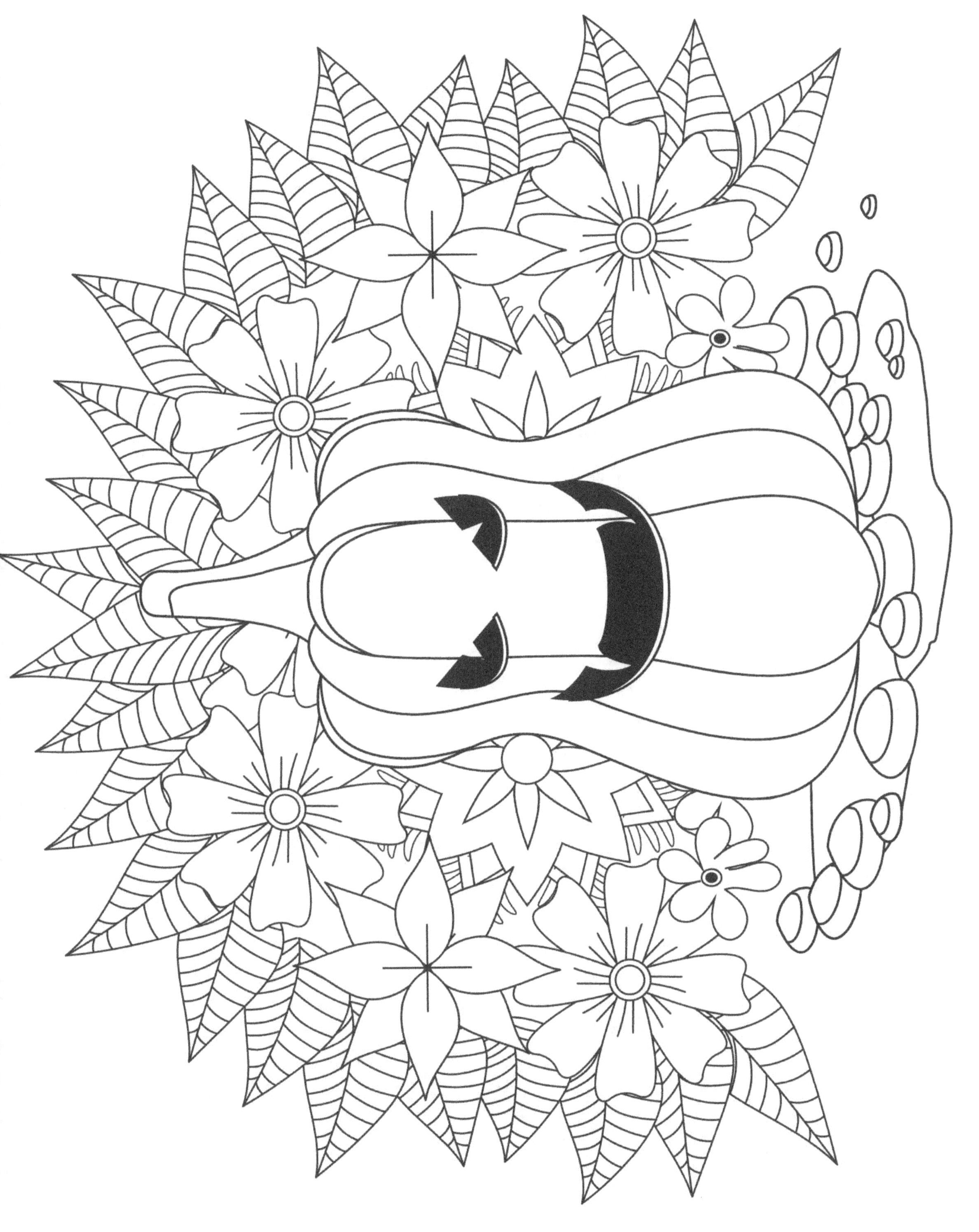

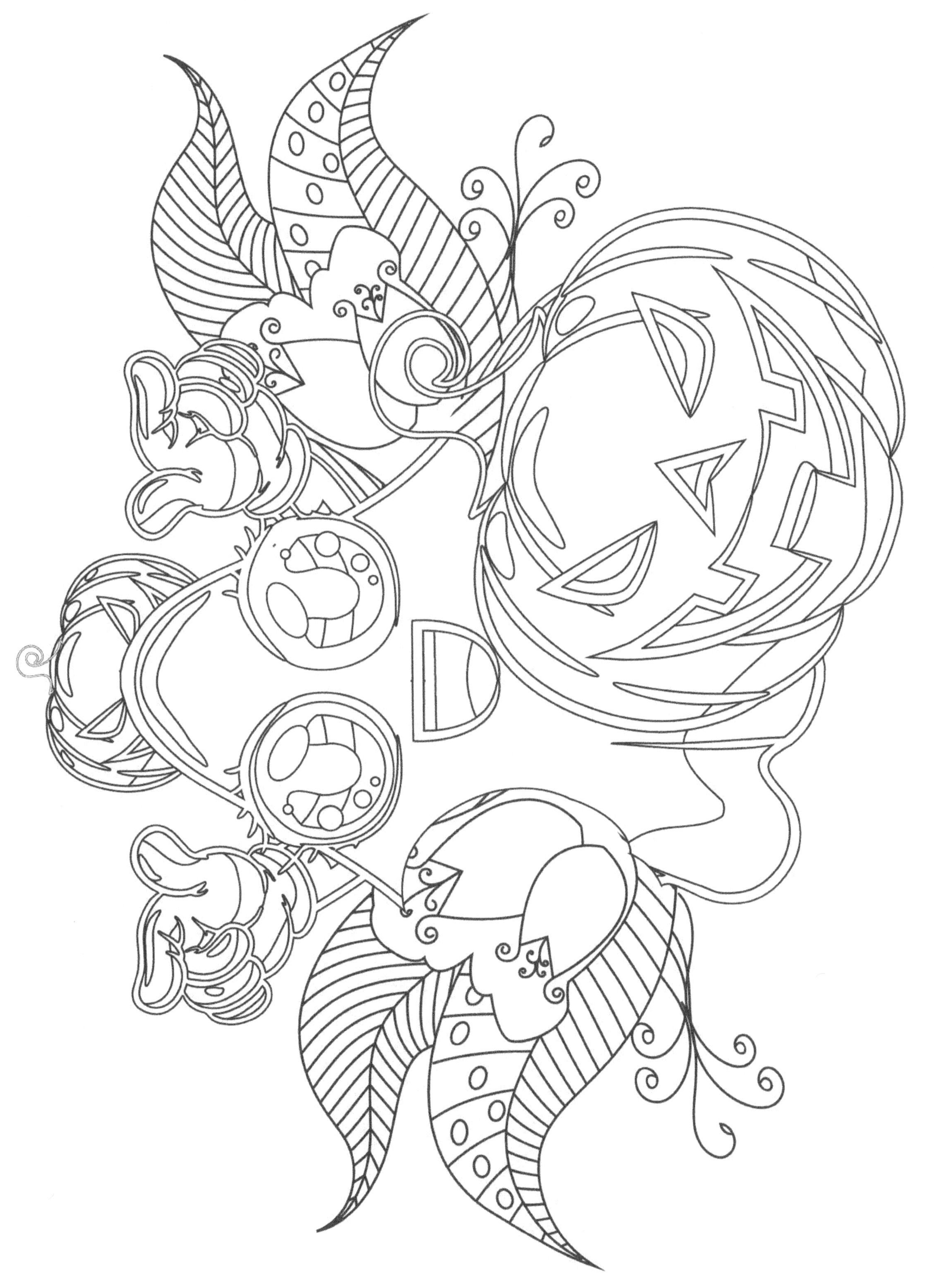

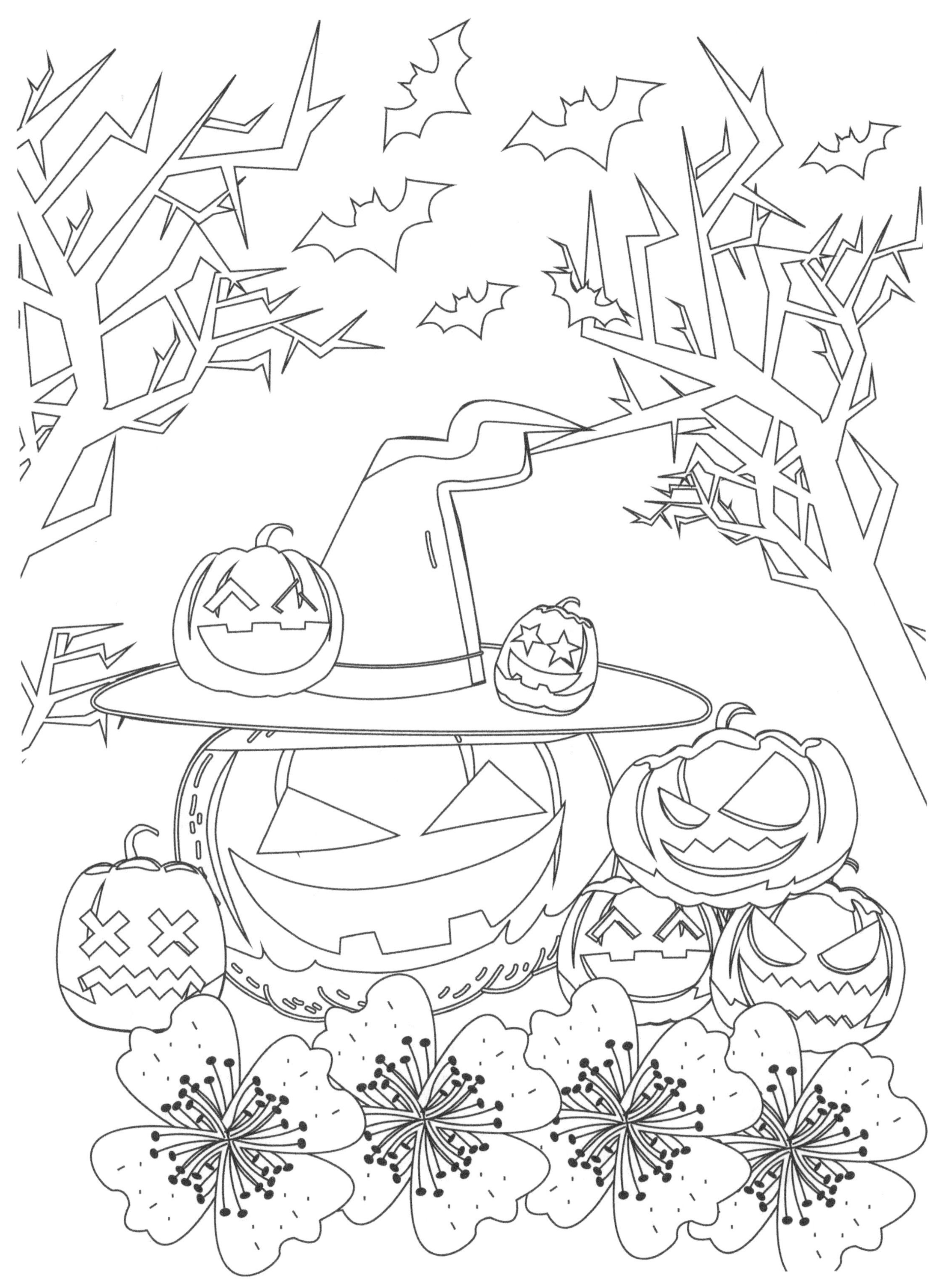

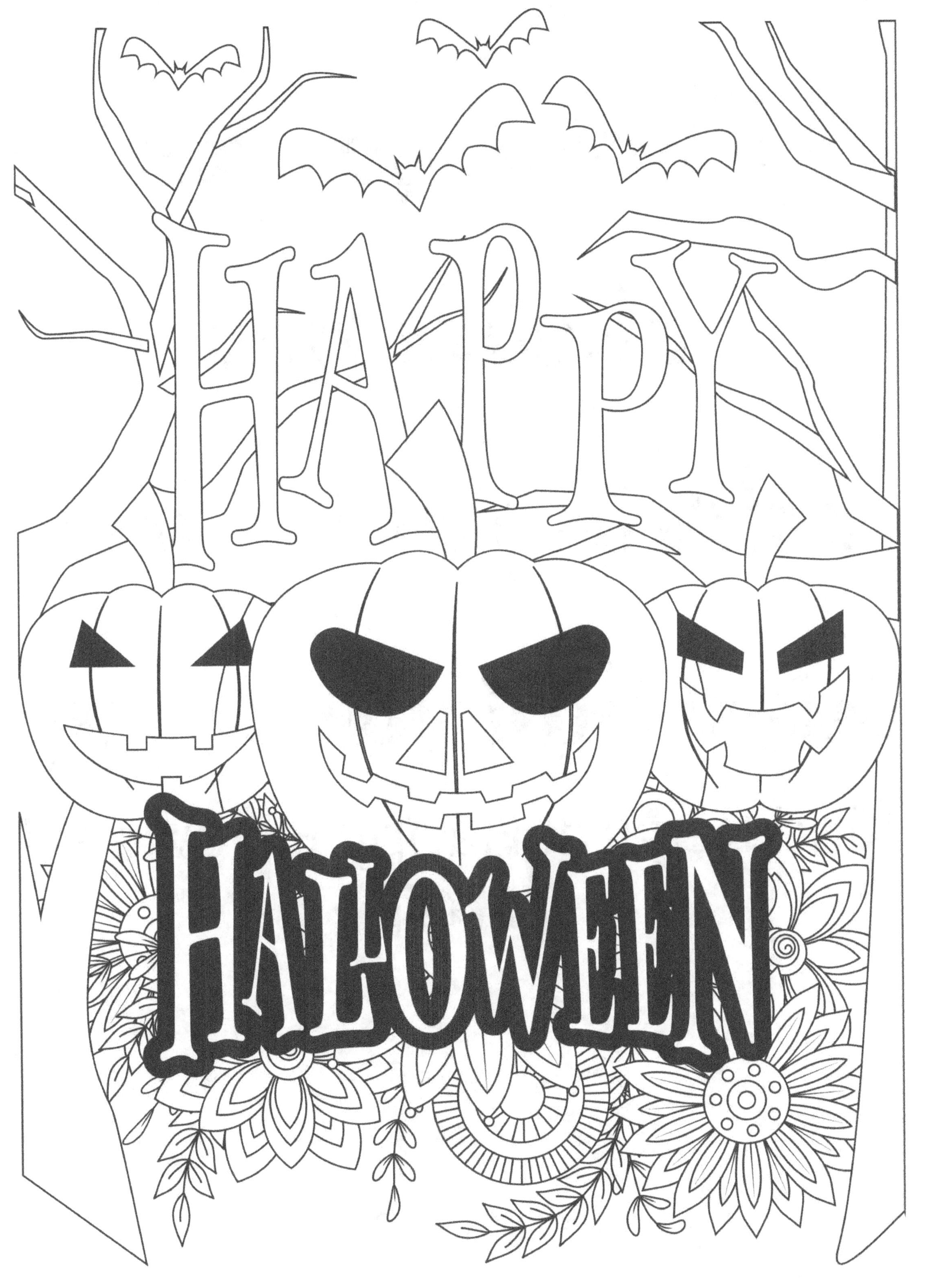
HAPPY
HALLOWEEN

Thank you for
choose this
coloring book. We
hope that you enjoy
Kind Regard! Happy Haloween!
that

Canada Quattro 2021

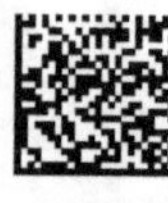